There Was a Young Man from Nantucket

1,001 LEWD LIMERICKS GUARANTEED TO AMUSE AND OFFEND

RONALD STANZA

Skyhorse Publishing

Reprinted by arrangement with Kensington Publishing Corp.

Skyhorse Publishing books may be purchased in bulk at special discounts for sales promotion, corporate gifts, fund-raising, or educational purposes. Special editions can also be created to specifications. For details, contact the Special Sales Department, Skyhorse Publishing, 307 West 36th Street, 11th Floor, New York, NY 10018 or info@skyhorsepublishing.com.

Skyhorse® and Skyhorse Publishing® are registered trademarks of Skyhorse Publishing, Inc.®, a Delaware corporation.

Visit our website at www.skyhorsepublishing.com.

10 9 8 7 6 5 4 3

Library of Congress Cataloging-in-Publication Data is available on file for the hardcover.

Cover design by Brian Peterson

Paperback ISBN: 978-1-63220-678-7
Ebook ISBN: 978-1-62087-341-0

Printed in the United States of America

CONTENTS

CONTENTS

I

Romance

There was a young girl of Aberystwyth
Who took grain to the mill to get grist with.
    The miller's son, Jack,
    Laid her flat on her back,
And united the organs they pissed with.

          There was a young lady of Arden,
          The tool of whose swain wouldn't harden.
               Said she with a frown,
                 "I've been sadly let down
               By the tool of a fool in a garden."

There once was a yokel of Beaconsfield
Engaged to look after the deacon's field,
    But he lurked in the ditches
    And diddled the bitches
Who happened to cross that antique 'un's field.

There's a charming young lady named Beaulieu
Who's often been screwed by yours truly,
    But now—it's appallin'—
    My balls always fall in!
I fear that I've fucked her unduly.

There was a young girl in Berlin
Who was fucked by an elderly Finn.
    Though he diddled his best,
    And fucked her with zest,
She kept asking, "Hey, Pop, is it in?"

I wooed a stewed nude in Bermuda,
I was lewd, but my God! she was lewder.
    She said it was crude
    To be wooed in the nude—
I pursued her, subdued her, and screwed her!

There was a young lady of Bicester
Who was nicer by far than her sister.
    The sister would giggle
    And wiggle and jiggle,
But this one would come if you kissed her.

There once was a son-of-a-bitch,
Neither clever, nor handsome, nor rich,
   Yet the girls he would dazzle
   And fuck to a frazzle,
And then ditch them, the son-of-a-bitch!

There was a young fellow named Blaine,
And he screwed some disgusting old jane.
   She was ugly and smelly,
   With an awful pot-belly,
But . . . well, they were caught in the rain.

There was a young sailor from Brighton
Who remarked to his girl, "You're a tight one."
   She replied, "'Pon my soul,
   You're in the wrong hole;
There's plenty of room in the right one."

A lacklustre lady of Brougham
Weaveth all night at her loom.
   Anon she doth blench
   When her lord and his wench
Pull a chain in the neighbouring room.

A middle-aged codger named Bruin
Found his love life completely a ruin,
For he flirted with flirts
Wearing pants and no skirts,
And he never got in for no screwin'.

There was a young fellow of Burma
Whose betrothed had good reason to murmur.
But now that he's married he's
Been using cantharides,
And the root of their love is much firmer.

There was a young fellow from Cal.,
In bed with a passionate gal.
He leapt from the bed,
To the toilet he sped;
Said the gal, "What about me, old pal?"

There was a young man from Calcutta
Who was heard in his beard to mutter,
"If her Bartholin glands
Don't respond to my hands,
I'm afraid I shall have to use butter."

There once was a kiddie named Carr
Caught a man on top of his mar.
    As he saw him stick 'er,
    He said with a snicker,
"You do it much faster than par."

There was a young fellow named Charteris
Put his hand where his young lady's garter is,
    Said she, "I don't mind,
    And up higher you'll find
The place where my fucker and farter is."

A young woman got married at Chester.
Her mother she kissed and she blessed her.
    Says she, "You're in luck;
    He's a stunning good fuck,
For I've had him myself down in Leicester."

"For the tenth time, dull Daphnis," said Chloe,
"You have told me my bosom is snowy;
    You have made much fine verse on
    Each part of my person,
Now *do* something—there's a good boy!"

A maiden who wrote of big cities
Some songs full of love, fun, and pities,
   Sold her stuff at the shop
   Of a musical wop
Who played with her soft little titties.

There once was a gouty old colonel
Who grew glum when the weather grew vernal,
   And he cried in his tiffin
   For his prick wouldn't stiffen,
And the size of the thing was infernal.

A lady while dining at Crewe,
Found an elephant's whang in her stew.
   Said the waiter, "Don't shout,
   And don't wave it about,
   Or the others will all want one too."

There was a young lady of Dee
Who went down to the river to pee.
   A man in a punt
   Put his hand on her cunt,
And God! how I wish it were me.

I never have had Miss Defauw,
But it wouldn't have been quite so raw
   If she'd only said "No"
   When I wanted her so;
But she didn't—she laughed and said "Naw!"

A beautiful belle of Del Norte
Is reckoned disdainful and haughty
   Because during the day
   She says: "Boys, keep away!"
But she fucks in the gloaming like forty.

A young man by a girl was desired;
To give her the thrills she required,
   But he died of old age
   Ere his cock could assuage
The volcanic desire it inspired.

There was a young lady of Dover
Whose passion was such that it drove her
   To cry when you came:
   "Oh dear! What a shame!
Well, now we shall have to start over."

There was a young man of Dumfries
Who said to his girl, "If you please,
 It would give me great bliss
 If, while playing with this,
You would pay some attention to these!"

There was a young lady of Ealing,
And her lover before her was kneeling.
 Said she, "Dearest Jim,
 Take your hand off my quim;
I much prefer fucking to feeling."

A lonely young lad of Eton
Used always to sleep with the heat on,
 Till he ran into a lass
 Who showed him her ass—
Now they sleep with only a sheet on.

There was a young lady of Exeter,
So pretty that men craned their necks at her.
    One was even so brave
    As to take out and wave
The distinguishing mark of his sex at her.

      There was a young lady of fashion
      Who had oodles and oodles of passion.
        To her lover she said
        As they climbed into bed,
      "Here's one thing the bastards can't ration!"

There was a young girl in Dakota
Had a letter from Ickes; he wrote her,
    "In addition to gas
    We are rationing ass,
And you've greatly exceeded your quota."

There was a young lady named Flynn
Who thought fornication a sin,
　　But when she was tight,
　　It seemed quite all right,
So everyone filled her with gin.

A reckless young lady of France
Had no qualms about taking a chance,
　　But she thought it was crude
　　To get screwed in the nude,
So she always went home with damp pants.

A nervous young fellow named Fred
Took a charming young widow to bed.
　　When he'd diddled a while,
　　She remarked with a smile,
"You've got it all in but the head."

There was a young fellow named Fyfe
Whose marriage was ruined for life,
  For he had an aversion
  To every perversion
And only liked fucking his wife.

Well, one year the poor woman struck,
And she wept, and she cursed at her luck,
  And said, "Where have you gotten us
  With your goddamn monotonous
Fuck after fuck after fuck?"

"I once knew a harlot named Lou—
And a versatile girl she was, too.
  After ten years of whoredom
  She perished of boredom
When she married a jackass like you!"

There was a young lady of Gloucester
Met a passionate fellow who tossed her.
   She wasn't much hurt,
   But he dirtied her skirt,
So think of the anguish it cost her.

There was a young lady of Gloucester
Whose friends they thought they had lost her,
   Till they found on the grass
   The marks of her arse
And the knees of the man who had crossed her.

There was a young fellow named Goody
Who claimed that he wouldn't, but would he?
   If he found himself nude
   With a gal in the mood,
The question's not would he but could he?

In my sweet little Alice Blue gown
Was the first time I ever laid down.
   I was both proud and shy
    As he opened his fly,
And the moment I saw it I thought I would die.

        Oh it hung almost down to the ground.
        As it went in I made not a sound.
           The more that he shoved it,
           The more that I loved it
        As he came on my Alice Blue gown.

In my sweet little night gown of blue,
On the first night that I slept with you,
   I was both shy and scared
    As the bed was prepared,
And you played peekaboo with my ribbons of blue.

As we both watched the break of day,
And in peaceful submission I lay,
    You said you adored it,
    But dammit, you tore it,
My sweet little nightgown of blue.

Winter is here with his grouch,
The time when you sneeze and slouch.
    You can't take your women
    Canoein' or swimmin',
But a lot can be done on a couch.

It always delights me at Hanks
To walk up the old riverbanks.
    One time in the grass
    I stepped on an ass
And heard a young girl murmur, "Thanks."

There was a young girl from Hong Kong
Who said, "You are utterly wrong
   To say my vagina's the largest in China,
Just because of your mean little dong."

        There was once a sad Maïtre d'hŏtel
        Who said: "They can all go to hell!
           What they do to my wife—
           Why, it ruins my life;
        And the worst is, they all do it well."

There was a young man named Hughes
Who swore off all kinds of booze.
   He said, "When I'm muddled
   My senses get fuddled,
And I pass up too many screws."

There were three ladies of Huxham,
And whenever we meets 'em we fucks 'em,
   And when that game grows stale,
   We sits on a rail
And pulls out our pricks, and they sucks 'em.

There was a young lady named Inge
Who went on a binge with a dinge.
   Now I won't breathe a word
   Of what really occurred—
But her cunt has a chocolate fringe.

An octogenarian Jew
To his wife remained steadfastly true.
   This was not from compunction
   But due to dysfunction
Of his spermatic glands—nuts to you.

"Snyder's got a stiff ticket," said Kay,
"Come on, take it out, and let's play."
    He pulled it on out,
    But she started to pout,
His ticket was only a quarter-inch stout.

    A pansy who lived in Khartoum
    Took a lesbian up to his room,
        And they argued all night
        Over who had the right
    To do what and with which and to whom.

2

Organs

In the Garden of Eden lay Adam,
Complacently stroking his madam,
    And loud was his mirth
    For on all of the earth
There were only two balls—and he had 'em.

        There was a young bride of Antigua
        Whose husband said, "Dear me, how big you are!"
            Said the girl: "What damn'd rot!
            Why, you've felt my twot,
        My legs and my arse and my figua!"

There was a young damsel named Baker
Who was poked in a pew by a Quaker.
    He yelled: "My God! What
    Do you call this—a twat?
Why, the entrance is more than an acre!"

There was once a mechanic named Bench
Whose best tool was a sturdy gut-wrench.
   With this vibrant device
   He could reach, in a trice,
The innermost parts of a wench.

There was a young man of Bengal
Who swore he had only one ball,
   But two little bitches
   Unbuttoned his britches
And found he had no balls at all.

A chippy who worked in Black Bluff
Had a pussy as large as a muff.
   It had room for both hands
   And some intimate glands
And was soft as a little duck's fluff.

There was a young lady named Blount
Who had a rectangular cunt.
   She learned for diversion
   Posterior perversion,
Since no one could fit her in front.

There was a young fellow named Bowen
Whose pecker kept growin' and growin'.
　　It grew so tremendous,
　　So long and so pendulous,
'Twas no good for fuckin'—just showin'.

There was a young lady named Brent
With a cunt of enormous extent,
　　And so deep and so wide,
　　The acoustics inside
Were so good you could hear when you spent.

There was a young girl from the Bronix
Who had a vagina of onyx.
　　She had so much tsoris
　　With her clitoris,
She traded it in for a Packard.

There was a young lady from Brussels
Who was proud of her vaginal muscles.
　　She could easily plex them
　　And so interflex them
As to whistle love songs through her bustles.

There was a young lady of Bude
Who walked down the street in the nude.
　　A bobby said, "Whattum
　　Magnificent bottom!"
And slapped it as hard as he could.

There once was a queen of Bulgaria
Whose bush had grown hairier and hairier,
　Till a prince from Peru
　Who came up for a screw
Had to hunt for her cunt with a terrier.

There was a young girl of Cah'lina,
Had a very capricious vagina:
　　To the shock of the fucker
　　'Twould suddenly pucker,
And whistle the chorus of "Dinah."

A lady with features cherubic
Was famed for her area pubic.
　When they asked her its size
　She replied in surprise,
"Are you speaking of square feet or cubic?"

There was a fat lady of China
Who'd a really enormous vagina,
    And when she was dead,
    They painted it red
And used it for docking a liner.

I met a young man in Chungking
Who had a very long thing—
    But you'll guess my surprise
    When I found that its size
Just measured a third-finger ring!

There was a young man of Coblenz
Whose ballocks were simply immense:
    It took forty-four draymen,
    A priest, and three laymen
To carry them thither and thence.

There was an old man of Connaught
Whose prick was remarkably short.
    When he got into bed
    The old woman said,
"This isn't a prick, it's a wart."

There once was a girl from Cornell
Whose teats were shaped like a bell.
   When you touched them they shrunk,
   Except when she was drunk,
And then they got bigger than hell.

There once was a lady of Crete
So enormously broad in the beam
   That one day in the ocean
   She caused such commotion
That Admiral Byrd claimed her for America.

There was a young fellow named Cribbs
Whose cock was so big it had ribs.
   They were inches apart,
   And to suck it took art,
While to fuck it took forty-two trips.

There was a young lady whose cunt
Could accommodate a small punt.
   Her mother said, "Annie,
   It matches your fanny,
Which never was that of a runt."

There's a young Yiddish slut with two cunts,
Whose pleasure in life is to pruntz.
　　When one pireg is shot,
　　There's that, alternate twat,
But the ausgefuckt male merely grunts.

There was a young man from Dallas
Who had an exceptional phallus.
　　He couldn't find room
　　In any girl's womb
Without rubbing it first with Vitalis.

There was a young girl of Des Moines
Whose cunt could be fitted with coins,
　　Till a guy from Hoboken
　　Went and dropped in a token,
And now she rides free on the ferry.

To his bride said the keen-eyed detective:
"Can it be that my eyesight's defective?
　　Has the east tit the least bit
　　The best of the west tit,
Or is it the faulty perspective?"

There was a young girl of Detroit
Who at fucking was very adroit:
   She could squeeze her vagina
   To a pin-point, or finer,
Or open it out like a quoit.

And she had a friend named Durand
Whose cock could contract or expand.
   He could diddle a midge
   Or the arch of a bridge—
Their performance together was grand!

There was a young man of Devizes
Whose balls were of different sizes.
   His tool, when at ease,
   Hung down to his knees.
Oh, what must it be when it rises!

Visas erat: huic geminarum
Dispar modus testicularum:
   Minor haec nihili,
   Palma triplici,
Jam fecerat altera clarum.

There was a young fellow whose dong
Was prodigiously massive and long.
  On each side of this whang
  Two testes did hang
That attracted a curious throng.

There was a young man from East Wubley
Whose cock was bifurcated doubly.
  Each quadruplicate shaft
  Had two balls hanging aft,
And the general effect was quite lovely.

While I, with my unusual enthusiasm,
Was exploring in Ermintrude's busiasm,
  She explained, "They are flat,
  But think nothing of that—
You will find that my sweet sister Susiasm."

There was a young fellow from Florida
Who liked a friend's wife, so he borrowed her.
  When they got into bed,
  He cried: "God strike me dead!
This ain't a cunt—it's a corridor!"

An old man at the Folies Bergère
Had a jock, a most wondrous affair:
    It snipped off a twat-curl
    From each new chorus girl,
And he had a wig made of the hair.

There was a young man with one foot
Who had a very long root.
    If he used this peg
    As an extra leg
Is a question exceedingly moot.

In the case of a lady named Frost,
Whose cunt's a good two feet acrost,
    It's the best part of valor
    To bugger the gal, or
You're apt to fall in and get lost.

A certain young person of Ghent,
Uncertain if lady or gent,
    Shows his organs at large
    For a small handling charge
To assist him in paying the rent.

        There was an old woman of Ghent
        Who swore that her cunt had no scent.
            She got fucked so often
            At last she got rotten,
        And didn't she stink when she spent.

There was a young man from Glengozzle
Who found a remarkable fossil.
    He knew by the bend
    And the wart on the end,
'Twas the peter of Paul the Apostle.

There was a young fellow of Greenwich
Whose balls were all covered with spinach.
    He had such a tool
    It was wound on a spool,
And he reeled it out inch by inch.

But this tale has an unhappy finich,
For due to the sand in the spinach
    His ballocks grew rough
    And wrecked his wife's muff,
And scratched up her thatch in the scrimmage.

A mathematician named Hall
Had a hexahedronical ball,
    And the cube of its weight
    Times his pecker plus eight
Was four-fifths of five-eights of fuck-all.

There was a young fellow of Harrow
Whose John was the size of a marrow.
   He said to his tart:
   "How's this for a start?
My balls are outside in a barrow."

     There was a young fellow named Harry,
     Had a joint that was long, huge, and scary.
        He pressed it on a virgin
         Who, without any urgin',
     Immediately spread like a fairy.

There was a young girl named Heather
Whose twitcher was made out of leather.
   She made a queer noise,
    Which attracted the boys,
By flapping the edges together.

There was an old curate of Hestion
Who'd erect at the slightest suggestion.
   But so small was his tool
   He could scarce screw a spool,
And a cunt was quite out of the question.

There was a young man from Hong Kong
Who had a trifurcated prong:
   A small one for sucking,
   A large one for fucking,
And a honey for beating a gong.

A fellow whose surname was Hunt
Trained his cock to perform a slick stunt:
   This versatile spout
   Could be turned inside out,
Like a glove, and be used as a cunt.

Alas for the Countess d'Isère,
Whose muff wasn't furnished with hair.
   Said the Count, "Quelle surprise!"
   When he parted her thighs;
"Magnifique! Pourtant pas de la guerre."

A highly aesthetic young Jew
Had eyes of a heavenly blue;
   The end of his dillie
   Was shaped like a lily,
And his balls were too utterly two!

There once was a lady from Kansas
Whose cunt was as big as Bonanzas.
   It was nine inches deep
   And the sides were quite steep—
It had whiskers like General Carranza's.

Oh, pity the Duchess of Kent!
Her cunt is so dreadfully bent,
   The poor wench doth stammer,
   "I need a sledgehammer
To pound a man into my vent."

There was an old gent from Kentuck
Who boasted a filigreed schmuck,
   But he put it away
   For fear that one day
He might put it in and get stuck.

There was an old lady of Kewry
Whose cunt was a lusus naturae:
   The introitus vaginae
   Was unnaturally tiny,
And the thought of it filled her with fury.

3

Intercourse

Thus spake I am that I am:
"For the Virgin I don't give a damn.
 What pleases Me most
 Is to bugger the Ghost,
And then be sucked off by the Lamb."

Así dije yo soy que yo soy:
"Por La Virgen un carajo no doy.
 Lo que debe gustar
 Es Jesús caporar—
Y para hacerlo Yo voy."

Dame Catherine of Ashton-on-Lynches
Got on with her grooms and her wenches:
 She went down on the gents
 And pronged the girls' vents
With a clitoris reaching six inches.

There was a young lady named Astor
Who never let any get past her.
    She finally got plenty
    By stopping twenty,
Which certainly ought to last her.

Oden the bardling averred
His muse was the bum of a bird,
    And his lesbian wife
    Would finger his fife
While Fisherwood waited as third.

There was a young fellow named Babbitt
Who could screw nine times like a rabbit,
    But a girl from Johore
    Could do it twice more,
Which was just enough extra to crab it.

A young polo-player of Berkeley
Made love to his sweetheart berserkly.
    In the midst of each chukker
    He would break off and fuck her
Horizontally, laterally, and verkeley.

There once was a jolly old bloke
Who picked up a girl for a poke.
  He took down her pants,
  Fucked her into a trance,
And then shit in her shoe for a joke.

There was a young idler named Blood,
Made a fortune performing at stud
  With a fifteen-inch peter,
  A double-beat metre,
And a load like the Biblical Flood.

Though the invalid Saint of Brac
Lay all of his life on his back,
  His wife got her share,
  And the pilgrims now stare
At the scene, in his shrine, on a plaque.

There was an old man of Brienz
The length of whose cock was immense:
  With one swerve he could plug
  A boy's bottom in Zug
And a kitchen-maid's cunt in Coblenz.

There once was a Duchess of Bruges
Whose cunt was incredibly huge.
    Said the king to this dame
    As he thunderously came:
"Mon Dieu! Après moi, le dèluge!"

There was an old man of Cajon
Who never could get a good bone.
    With the aid of a gland
    It grew simply grand;
Now his wife cannot leave it alone.

There was a young girl of Cape Cod
Who dreamt she'd been buggered by God.
    But it wasn't Jehovah
    That turned the girl over,
'Twas Roger the lodger, the dirty old codger,
The bugger, the bastard, the sod!

There once was a lady named Carter,
Fell in love with a virile young Tartar.
   She stripped off his pants,
    At his prick quickly glanced,
And cried, "For that I'll be a martyr!"

A talented fuckstress, Miss Chisholm,
Was renowned for her fine paroxysm.
   While the man detumesced,
    She still spent on with zest,
Her rapture sheer anachronism.

There was a young man in the choir
Whose penis rose higher and higher,
   Till it reached such a height
    It was quite out of sight—
But of course you know I'm a liar.

There was a young man from the Coast
Who had an affair with a ghost.
   At the height of orgasm
    Said the pallid phantasm,
"I think I can feel it—almost!"

Have you heard of the lady named Cox
Who had a capacious old box?
  When her lover was in place,
  She said: "Please turn your face.
I look like a gal, but I screw like a fox."

A team playing baseball in Dallas
Called the umpire a shit out of malice.
  While this worthy had fits,
  The team made eight hits
And a girl in the bleachers named Alice.

There was a young girl of Darjeeling
Who could dance with such exquisite feeling
  There was never a sound
  For miles around
Save of fly-buttons hitting the ceiling.

There was a young woman in Dee
Who stayed with each man she did see.
  When it came to a test
  She wished to be best,
And practice makes perfect, you see.

There was a family named Doe,
An ideal family to know.
   As father screwed mother,
   She said, "You're heavier than brother."
And he said, "Yes, Sis told me so!"

     A lady, by passion deluded,
     Found an African drunk and denuded,
       And—fit as a fiddle
       And hot for a diddle—
     She tied splints to his penis and screwed it.

There was a strong man of Drumrig
Who one day did seven times frig.
   He buggered three sailors,
   Four Jews, and two tailors,
And ended by fucking a pig.

     There was an old man of Duluth
     Whose cock was shot off in his youth.
       He fucked with his nose
       And with fingers and toes,
     And he came through a hole in his tooth.

There was an old man of Dundee
Who came home as drunk as could be.
    He wound up the clock
    With the end of his cock
And buggered his wife with the key.

    A rapturous young fellatrix
    One day was at work on five pricks.
        With an unholy cry
        She whipped out her glass eye:
    "Tell the boys I can now take on six."

There was a young man with a fiddle
Who asked of his girl, "Do you diddle?"
    She replied, "Yes, I do
    But prefer to with two—
It's twice as much fun in the middle."

    I dined with Lord Hughing Fitz-Bluing
    Who said, "Do you squirm when you're screwing?"
        I replied, "Simple shagging
        Without any wagging
    Is only for screwing canoeing."

There was a young fellow named Fletcher,
Was reputed an infamous lecher.
  When he'd take on a whore
  She'd need a rebore,
And they'd carry him out on a stretcher.

A young fellow discovered through Freud
That although of a penis devoid,
  He could practice coitus
  By eating a foetus,
And his parents were quite overjoyed.

There was a young man from Jodhpur
Who found he could easily cure
  His dread diabetes
  By eating a foetus
Served up in a sauce of manure.

There once was a sailor named Gasted.
A swell guy, as long as he lasted,
  He could jerk himself off
  In a basket, aloft,
Or a breeches-buoy swung from the masthead.

There was a young girl of Gibraltar
Who was raped as she knelt at the altar.
  It really seems odd
  That a virtuous God
Should answer her prayers and assault her.

      A young man with passions quite gingery
      Tore a hole in his sister's best lingerie.
        He slapped her behind
        And made up his mind
      To add incest to insult and injury.

A passionate red-headed girl,
When you kissed her, her senses would whirl,
  And her twat would get wet
  And would wiggle and fret,
And her cunt lips would curl and unfurl.

      There was a young lady named Gloria
      Who was had by Sir Gerald Du Maurier,
        And then by six men,
        Sir Gerald again,
      And the band at the Waldorf-Astoria.

Thank God for the Duchess of Gloucester,
She obliges all who accost her.
　　She welcomes the prick
　　Of Tom, Harry, or Dick,
Or Baldwin, or even Lord Astor.

The latest reports from Good Hope
State that apes there have pricks thick as rope
　　And fuck high, wide, and free
　　From the top of one tree
To the top of the next—what a scope!

A newlywed couple from Goshen
Spent their honeymoon sailing the ocean.
　　In twenty-eight days
　　They got laid eighty ways—
Imagine such fucking devotion!

There was a young fellow named Grimes
Who fucked his girl seventeen times
　　In the course of a week—
　　And this isn't to speak
Of assorted venereal crimes.

There was a young lady named Hatch
Who would always come through in a scratch.
    If a guy wouldn't neck her,
    She'd grab up his pecker
And shove the damn thing up her snatch.

There was a young lady named Hilda
Who went for a walk with a builder.
    He knew that he could,
    And he should, and he would—
And he did—and he goddamn near killed her!

I know of a fortunate Hindu
Who is sought in the towns that he's been to
    By the ladies he knows,
    Who are thrilled to the toes
By the tricks he can make his foreskin do.

If you're speaking of actions immoral,
Then how about giving the laurel
   To doughty Queen Esther;
   No three men could best her—
One fore, and one aft, and one oral.

There was a young miss from Johore
Who'd lie on a mat on the floor;
   In a manner uncanny
   She'd wobble her fanny
And drain your nuts dry to the core.

There was a young fellow of Kent
Whose prick was so long that it bent,
   So to save himself trouble
   He put it in double,
And instead of coming he went.

There was a young man of Kildare
Who was fucking a girl on the stair.
   The banister broke,
   But he doubled his stroke
And finished her off in midair.

      A young man of Llanfairpwllgwyngyll,
      While bent over plucking a dingle,
         Had the whole Eisteddfod
         Taking turns at his pod
      While they sang some impossible jingle.

There once were two brothers named Luntz
Who buggered each other at once.
   When asked to account
   For this intricate mount,
They said, "Assholes are tighter than cunts."

There was a young lady named Mable
Who liked to sprawl out on the table,
   Then cry to her man,
   "Stuff in all you can—
Get your ballocks in, too, if you're able."

An impotent Scot named MacDougall
Had to husband his sperm and be frugal.
   He was gathering semen
   To gender a he-man,
By screwing his wife through a bugle.

There once was a girl named McGoffin
Who was diddled amazingly often.
   She was rogered by scores
   Who'd been turned down by whores,
And was finally screwed in her coffin.

A stout Gaelic warrior, McPherson,
Was having a captive, a person
    Who was not averse
    Though she had the curse,
And he'd breeches of bristling furs on.

There was a young Scot in Madrid
Who got fifty-five fucks for a quid.
    When they said, "Are you faint?"
    He replied, "No, I ain't,
But I don't feel as good as I did."

4

Oral Irregularity

There once was a lady from Arden
Who sucked off a man in a garden.
He said, "My dear Flo,
Where does all that stuff go?"
And she said, "(swallowed hard)—I beg pardon?"

Said a man to a maid of Ashanti,
"Can one sniff of your twitchet, or can't he?"
Said she with a grin:
"Sure, shove your nose in!
But presto, please—not too andante."

There was a young fellow of Buckingham,
Wrote a treatise on cunts and on sucking them,
But later this work
Was eclipsed by a Turk
Whose topic was assholes and fucking them.

There was a young girl in Berlin
Who eked out a living through sin.
   She didn't mind fucking
   But much preferred sucking,
And she'd wipe off the pricks on her chin.

A fastidious young fop of Bhogat
Would suck a girl's cunt, just like that,
   But he'd wipe off her jib,
   And then slip on a bib,
To make sure not to soil his cravat.

There was a young lass of Blackheath
Who frigged an old man with her teeth.
   She complained that he stunk—
   Not so much from the spunk,
But his arsehole was just underneath.

An explorer whose habits were blunt
Once flavored some cannibal cunt.
   The asshole was shitty,
   And—more was the pity—
It oozed from the rear to the front.

In his youth our old friend Boccaccio
Was having a girl in a patio.
When it came to the twat,
She wasn't so hot,
But, boy, was she good at fellatio!

There was an old fellow of Brest
Who sucked off his wife with a zest.
Despite her great howls,
He sucked out her bowels
And spat them all over her chest.

There was a young fairy named Bates
Who took out young fellows on dates.
With his hands on their hips
He applied his hot lips
To their phalluses, testes, and nates.

There was a young bride, a Canuck,
Told her husband: "Let's do more than suck.
You say that I, maybe,
Can have my first baby—
Let's give up this Frenching and fuck!"

King Louis gave a lesson in class,
One time he was sexing a lass.
    When she used the word "Damn,"
    He rebuked her, "Please ma'am,
Keep a more civil tongue in my ass."

There was an old bugger of Como
Who suddenly cried, "Ecce homo!"
    He tracked his man down
    To the heart of the town
And gobbled him off in the duomo.

A fellatrix's healthful condition
Proved the value of spunk as nutrition.
    Her remarkable diet
    (I suggest that you try it)
Was only her clients' emission.

A pert miss named Mary Contrary
Was attacked by a man on a ferry.
    When he'd done, he said, "Come
    On now, swallow my scum!"
"I won't—but I want to," said Mary.

There was a young man named Isaac Cox
Who took as his motto, "I suck cocks."
    This frank declaration
    Brought him such reputation
That he spent twenty years sucking cocks
on the docks.

A girl with a sebaceous cyst
Always came when her asshole was kissed.
    Her lover was gratified
    That she was so satisfied,
But regretted the fun that he missed.

The nephew of one of the czars
Used to suck off Rasputin at Yars,
    Till the peasants revolted,
    The royal family bolted—
Now they're under the sickle and stars.

There once was a cuntlapper's daughter
Who, despite all her father had taught her,
    Would become so unstrung
    At the touch of a tongue
That she'd deluge her beau with her water.

    There was an old man of Decatur,
    Took out his red-hot pertater.
        He tried at her dent,
        But when his thing bent,
    He got down on his knees and he ate 'er.

There once was a maid in Duluth,
A striver and seeker of truth.
    This pretty wench
    Was adept at French,
And said all else was uncouth.

    A progressive and young Eskimo
    Grew tired of his squaw and so
        Slipped out of his hut
        To look for a slut
    Who knew the very fine art of blow.

There was a young lady named Grace
Who took all she could in her face,
    But an adequate lad
    Gave her all that he had,
And blew tonsils all over the place.

That naughty old Sappho of Greece
Said, "What I prefer to a piece
    Is to have my pudenda
    Rubbed hard by the enda
The little pink nose of my niece."

There was a young Jewess named Hannah
Who sucked off her lover's banana.
    She swore that the cream
    That shot out in a stream
Tasted better than Biblical manna.

There was a young lady named Hix
Who was fond of sucking big pricks.
    One fellow she took
    Was a doctor named Snook.
Now he's in a hell of a fix.

A Roman of old named Horatio
Was fond of a form of fellatio.
   He kept accurate track
   Of the boys he'd attack,
And called it his cock-sucking ratio.

     The priests at the temple of Isis
     Used to offer up amber and spices,
       Then back of the shrine
       They would play 69
     And other unmentionable vices.

There was an old man from Keith
Who never could get any pieth
   By asking young men
   If they hadn't the yen
To get sucked off by one without teeth.

     There was a young bounder named Link
     Who possessed a very tart dink.
       To sweeten it some
       He steeped it in rum,
     And he's driven the ladies to drink.

There lived in French Louisiana
A quaint and deceived old duenna
    Who naively thought
    That a penis was wrought
To be et like a thick ripe banana.

There was an old maid from Luck
Who took it into her head to fuck.
    She was about to resign
    Till she hung out a sign:
"Come in, I've decided to suck."

Aren't you a trifle atavistic, Mac,
With that little supernumerary nipple on your sac?
    When I go down to eat,
    My purpose I defeat
When my lips slip from meat to teat and back.

A canny Scotch lass named McFargle,
Without coaxing and such argy-bargle,
    Would suck a man's pud
    Just as hard as she could,
And she saved up the sperm for a gargle.

Said the priest to Miss Bridget McLennin,
"Sure, a kiss of your twat isn't sinnin'."
    And he stuck to this story
    Till he tasted the gory
And menstruous state she was then in.

    A Lesbian lady named Maud
    Got into the Wacs by a fraud.
       With a tongue long and knobby
       She raped Col. Hobby,
    And now she's a major, by god!

There was a young fellow named Meek
Who invented a lingual technique.
    It drove women frantic
    And made them romantic,
And wore all the hair off his cheek.

    "It's dull in Duluth, Minnesota,
    Of spirit there's not an iota,"
       Complained Alice to Joe,
       Who tried not to show
    That he yawned in her snatch as he blowed her.

There was a young man of Nantucket
Whose prick was so long he could suck it.
    He said with a grin,
    As he wiped off his chin,
"If my ear were a cunt, I could fuck it."

        A socialite out on Nantucket
        Had a twat that was wide as a bucket.
           She proclaimed, "If it's clean,
           I will take it between;
        If it's rotten, I'd far better suck it."

There once was an Anglican pastor
Whose maid didn't let much get past her.
    She said, "When you muffdive on
    The living-room divan,
Please use an antimacassar."

        There was a young fellow named Pell
        Who didn't like cunt very well.
           He would finger and fuck one,
           But never would suck one—
        He just couldn't get used to the smell.

There once was a brilliant young poet
Who loved it—wouldn't you know it?
    When you'd want to sixty-nine
    His penis would pine.
"I just can't," it said. "I can't go it."

    "At a séance," said a young man named Post,
    "I was being sucked off by a ghost;
        Someone switched on the lights,
        And there in gauze tights,
    On his knees, was Tobias mine host."

There was a young dancer, Priscilla,
Who flavored her cunt with vanilla.
    The taste was so fine,
    Men and beasts stood in line,
Including a stud armadilla.

An old doctor who lacked protoplasm
Tried to give his young wife an orgasm,
    But his tongue jumped the track
    'Twixt the front and the back.
And got pinched in a bad anal spasm.

There was a young man of Saint Kitts
Who was very much troubled with fits.
    After chewing a gal's cunt,
    He'd give a loud grunt
And try to bite off her two teats.

A young bride was once heard to say:
"Oh dear, I am wearing away!
    The insides of my thighs
    Look just like mince pies,
For my husband won't shave every day."

There was a young man of Soho
Whose tastes were exceedingly low.
   He said to his mother,
    "Let us suck one another
And swallow the seminal flow."

      An Indian squaw up at Spruce
      Was unable to have a papoose.
         She said to her pater,
          When he asked, "What's the matter?"
      "I can't swallow the foul, slimy juice."

A worried young man from Stamboul
Discovered red spots on his tool.
   Said the doctor, a cynic:
    "Get out of my clinic!
Just wipe off the lipstick, you fool."

A tidy young lady of Streator
Dearly loved to nibble a peter.
　　She always would say:
　　"I prefer it this way.
I think it is very much neater."

Old Louis Quatorze was hot stuff.
He tired of that game, blindman's buff,
　　Up-ended his mistress,
　　Kissed hers while she kissed his,
And thus taught the world soixante-neuf.

There's a dowager near Sweden Landing
Whose manners are odd and demanding.
　　It's one of her jests
　　To suck off her guests—
She hates to keep gentlemen standing.

There was a young girl, very sweet,
Who thought sailors' meat quite a treat.
    When she sat on their lap
    She unbuttoned their flap,
And always had plenty to eat.

5

Buggery

There was a young man from Axminster
Whose designs were quite base and quite sinister.
   His lifelong ambition
   Was anal coition
With the wife of the French foreign minister.

       Berries, berries, all kinds of berries,
       Chancres on her ass like California cherries.
         The first time I hit her,
         I nearly broke her shitter
       Down where the Hasiampa flows.

There was a young man of Arras
Who stretched himself out on the grass,
   And with no little trouble
   He bent himself double
And stuck his prick well up his ass.

A convict once, out in Australia,
Said unto his turnkey, "I'll tail yer."
    But he said, "You be buggered,
    You filthy old sluggard,
You're forgetting as I am your gaoler."

A whimsical Arab from Aden,
His masculine member well laden,
    Cried, "Nuptial joy,
    When shared with a boy,
Is better than melon or maiden!"

A young man who lived in Balbriggan
Went to sea to recover from frigging,
    But after a week,
    As they climbed the forepeak,
He buggered the mate in the rigging.

A pederast living in Arles
Used to bugger the bung of a barrel
   But was heard to lament,
   "In the old days I went
Up the blue-blooded bum of an earl!"

     There was a young party of Bicester
     Who wanted to bugger his sister,
        But not liking dirt,
        He bought him a squirt
     And cleaned out her arse with a clyster.

Some night when you're drunk on Dutch Bols
Try changing the usual roles.
   The backward position
   Is nice for coition,
And it offers the choice of two holes.

There was a young belle from Bombay
Who never had thought herself gay,
   Till a queen from Siam
   Said, "My dear, you're not jam!"
And brought that one out right away.

There was a brave damsel of Brighton
Whom nothing could possibly frighten.
   She plunged in the sea
   And, with infinite glee,
Was fucked in the ass by a Triton.

As he lay in his bath, mused Lord Byng:
"Oh Blimy! What memories you bring!
   That gorgeous young trooper . . .
   No! No! Gladys Cooper!
By Gad, sir! That was a near thing."

Coitus upon a cadaver
Is the ultimate way you can have 'er.
   Her inanimate state
   Means a man needn't wait,
And eliminates all the palaver.

There was a young man of Calcutta
Who thought he would do a smart trick,
So anointed his arsehole with butter,
And in it inserted his prick.
It was not for greed after gold,
It was not for thirst after pelf;
'Twas simply because he'd been told
To bloody well bugger himself.

A Phi Delt known as Carruthers
Will never make little girls mothers.
Around the old brown
He is covered with down
To wipe off the dongs of his brothers.

There was a young man from Chubut
Who had a remarkable root:
When hard, it would bend
With a curve at the end,
So he fucked himself in the petoot.

A parson who lived near Cremorne
Looked down on all women with scorn.
   E'en a boy's white, fat bum
   Could not make him come,
But an old man's piles gave him the horn.

There was a fellow named Dave
Who kept a dead whore in a cave.
   He said, "I admit
   I'm a bit of a shit,
But think of the money I save!"

A mortician who practised in Fife
Made love to the corpse of his wife.
   "How could I know, Judge?
   She was cold, did not budge—
Just the same as she'd acted in life."

A glutted debauchee from Frome
Lured beauteous maids to his room,
   Where, after he'd strip 'em,
   He'd generally whip 'em
With a bundle of twigs or a broom.

When she wanted a new way to futter
He greased her behind with butter;
   Then, with a sock,
   In went his jock,
And they carried her home on a shutter.

     There was a young pansy named Gene
     Who cruised a sadistic Marine.
        Said the man with a smirk
        As they got down to work,
     "In this game the Jack beats the Queen."

There was a young lady of Glasgow,
And fondly her lover did ask, "Oh,
   Pray allow me a fuck,"
   But she said, "No, my duck,
But you may, if you please, up my arse go."

At the Iphigenia of Gluck
Two ushers attempted to fuck.
    At the blare of the brass
    One contracted his ass,
And they carted him off in a truck.

There was an old man named Grasty
Whose favorite sport was ass-ty.
    He'd bugger with joy
    Any innocent boy
But thought fornication was nasty.

A native of Havre de Grace
Once tired of cunt, said, "I'll try arse."
    He unfolded his plan
    To another young man,
Who said, "Most decidedly, my arse!"

There was a young fellow named Howell
Who buggered himself with a trowel.
    The triangular shape
    Was conducive to rape
And was easily cleaned with a towel.

A prisoner in Chateau d'If
Ran around on all fours for a sniff
   Of his comrade's posterior
   And said, "It's inferior,
But it somehow reminds me of quiff."

A Sultan of old Istanbul
Had a varicose vein in his tool.
   This evoked joyous grunts
   From his harem of cunts,
But his boys suffered pain at the stool.

Said an airy young fairy named Jess,
"The oral requires some finesse,
   While in method the anal
   Is terribly banal,
And the trousers will get out of press."

A psychiatrist fellow, quite Jung,
Asked his wife, "May I bugger your bung?"
   And was so much annoyed
   When he found her a-Freud,
He went out in the yard and ate dung.

There was a young reb from Kadoches
Who had a hospitable toches.
   His friends had no fear
   To attack from the rear,
For he'd make it quite kosher with broches.

An embalmer in ancient Karnak
Oozed it into a fresh corpse's crack.
   Rigor mortis set in
   And clamped off what had been
His pride, nor did he get it back.

There was a young fellow named Kelly
Who preferred his wife's ass to her belly.
   He shrieked with delight
   As he ploughed through the shite,
And filled up her hole with his jelly.

There was an old man of Kentucky,
Said to his old woman, "Oi'll fuck ye."
   She replied, "Now you wunt
   Come anigh my old cunt,
For your prick is all stinking and mucky."

There was an old phoney named Kinsey
Whose ideas of fucking were flimsy.
   He knew how to measure
   A penis for pleasure,
But he came much too quick in a quim, see?

There was a young man from Liberia
Who was forced to flee to the interior.
   He'd buggered a brother,
   His father and mother—
He considered his sisters inferior.

A youth who seduced a poor lighterman
Said, "I'd much sooner fuck than I'd fight a man,
   And although, Sir, I find
   You a very good grind,
I must say I've had a much tighter man."

There was a young mate of a lugger
Who took out a girl just to hug her.
   "I've my monthlies," she said,
   "And a cold in the head,
   But my bowels work well . . . Do you bugger?"

There was a young man of Madras
Who was having a boy in the grass.
  Then a cobra de capello
  Said, "Hello, young fellow!"
And bit a piece out of his arse.

There was a young priest from Madrid
Who looked with lewd eyes on a kid.
  He said: "With great joy
  I could bugger that boy.
I'll be damned if I don't!"—And he did.

There was a young lady whose mind
Was never especially refined.
  She got on her knees
  Her lover to please,
Who stuck in his prick from behind.

There once was a well-groomed young nance
Who responded to every advance,
    But rather than strip,
    He let anything slip
Through a hole in the seat of his pants.

There was a young man from Nantasket
Who screwed a dead whore in a casket.
    He allowed 'twas no vice
    But thought it was nice,
For she needed no money, nor'd ask it.

There was a young man from Nantucket
Who had such a big cock he could suck it.
    He looked in the glass
    And saw his own ass,
And broke his neck trying to fuck it.

Should a fellow discover some night
A girl's body in bed, it's all right.
   He should think it good luck,
   And accept the free fuck—
He will bugger her too, if he's bright.

There was a Captain of MAG 94
More easily had than a two-bit whore.
   He wanted to drink
   And fondle your dink,
But he's not around anymore.

There once was a doughty Norwegian
Who enlivened the French Foreign Legion,
   But his brothers-in-arms
   Who succumbed to his charms
All got clap in their hindermost region.

There was a young fellow named Oakum
Whose brags about fucking were hokum,
   For he really preferred
   To suck cocks and stir turd—
He was Queen of the Flits in Hoboken.

      Said Oscar McDingle O'Figgle
      With an almost hysterical giggle,
         "Last night I was sick
         With delight when my prick
      Felt dear Alfred's delicious arse wriggle!"

There was a young man of Oswego
Whose friends said, "Be off now, to sea go."
   He there learned the trick
   Of skinning his prick,
And up arses thrusting his pego.

A young queer who was much oversexed
Was easily fretted and vexed.
　　When out on a date,
　　He hardly could wait
To say, "Turn over, bud; my turn next."

There was an old man from Pinole
Who always got in the wrong hole,
　　And when he withdrew,
　　All covered with goo,
His temper was out of control.

A phenomenal fellow named Preston
Has a hair-padded lower intestine.
　　Though exceedingly fine
　　In the buggery line,
It isn't much good for digestin'.

6
Clergy Abuse

There was a young lady named Alice
Who peed in a Catholic chalice.
　　She said, "I do this
　　From a great need to piss,
And not from sectarian malice."

　　　　There were three young ladies of Birmingham,
　　　　And this is the scandal concerning 'em:
　　　　　　They lifted the frock
　　　　　　And tickled the cock
　　　　　　Of the bishop engaged in confirming 'em.

A modern monk nicknamed Augustin,
His penis a boy's bottom thrust in.
　　Then said Father Ignatius:
　　"Now really! Good gracious!
Your conduct is really disgusting."

There was a young pansy named Birch
Who developed a taste for the church,
   And monks, priests, and preachers,
   And such mouthy creatures,
Were the uplifted ends of his search.

There was a young girl in Alsace
Who was having her first piece of ass.
   "Oh, darling, you'll kill me!
   Oh, dearest, you thrill me
Like Father John's thumb after mass!"

Now, the bishop was nobody's fool,
He'd been to a good public school,
   So he took down their britches
   And buggered those bitches
With his ten-inch episcopal tool.

Then up spoke a lady from Kew,
And said, as the bishop withdrew,
   "The vicar is quicker
   And thicker and slicker
And longer and stronger than you."

There was a young bishop from Brest
Who openly practiced incest.
   "My sisters and nieces
   Are all dandy pieces,
And they don't cost a cent," he confessed.

There was a young curate of Buckingham
Who was blamed by the girls for not fucking 'em.
   He said: "Though my cock
   Is as hard as a rock,
Your cunts are too slack. Put a tuck in 'em."

There was a young lady of Cheyne
Who crept into the vestry unseen.
　　She pulled down her knickers,
　　And also the vicar's,
And said, "How about it, old bean?"

　　　　There was a young lady of Chichester
　　　　Who made all the saints in their niches stir.
　　　　　　One morning at matins
　　　　　　Her breasts in white satins
　　　　Made the Bishop of Chichester's britches stir.

A young curate, just new to the cloth,
At sex was surely no sloth.
　　He preached masturbation
　　To his whole congregation,
And was washed down the aisle on the froth.

I once had the wife of a dean
Seven times while the dean was out skiin'.
   She remarked with some gaiety,
   "Not bad for the laity,
Though the bishop once managed thirteen."

There was a young choirboy from Devon
Who was raped in a haystack by seven
   High Anglican priests—
   (Lascivious beasts)—
For of such is the kingdom of heaven.

There was a young monk from Dundee
Who hung a nun's cunt on a tree.
   He grabbed her fair ass
   And performed a high mass
That even the Pope came to see.

There was a young curate of Eltham
Who wouldn't fuck girls, but he felt 'em.
    In lanes he would linger
    And play at stink-finger,
And scream with delight when he smelt 'em.

    A big Catholic layman named Fox
    Makes his living by sucking off cocks.
      In spells of depression
      He goes to confession,
    And jacks off the priest in his box.

The priest, a cocksucker named Sheen,
Is delighted their sins aren't seen.
    "Though God sees through walls,"
    Says Monsignor, "—Oh, balls!
This God stuff is simply a screen."

There was an archbishop in France
Who saw a nude woman by chance.
    The result, I affirm,
    Was emission of sperm
In the archiepiscopal pants.

There once was a priest of Gibraltar
Who wrote dirty jokes in his Psalter.
    An inhibited nun
    Who had read every one
Made a vow to be laid on his altar.

There was a young lady named Jessary
Got deflowered while in a confessary.
    The priest who thus wrecked her
    Would scorn a protector,
While she'd never heard of a pessary!

There was an old Abbot of Khief
Who thought the impenitent thief
   Had bollocks of brass
   And an amethyst arse.
He died in this awful belief.

       There was a young monk of Kilkyre,
       Was smitten with carnal desire.
          The immediate cause
          Was the abbess' drawers,
       Which were hung up to dry by the fire.

There was a young rector of Kings
Whose mind was on heavenly things,
   But his heart was on fire
   For a boy in the choir
Whose ass was like jelly on springs.

Apud Rege tutor veteramus
Fuellaria odit profanes
    Semper optandus
    Pueri sperandus
Gellifactus in siliis anus.

When a lecherous curate at Leeds
Was discovered, one day, in the weeds
    Astride a young nun,
    He said: "Christ, this is fun!
Far better than telling one's beads!"

A Sunday school student in Mass.
Soon rose to the head of the class
    By reciting quite night
    And by sleeping at night
With his tongue up the minister's ass.

In Kansas there lived a young monk
Who often was in a blue funk,
    For his come always froze
    On the sisters' thick hose,
And they never would part with a chunk.

    A lecherous Bishop of Peoria,
    In a state of constant euphoria,
        Enjoyed having fun
        With a whore or a nun
    While chanting the Sanctus and Gloria.

There was a gay rector of Poole
Most deservedly proud of his tool.
    With some trifling aid
    From the curate, 'tis said,
He rogered the National School.

A hoary old monk of Regina
Once said, "There is nothing diviner
   Than to sit in one's cell
   And let one's mind dwell
On the charms of the Virgin's vagina."

There was a young man of St. Giles
Who'd walked thousands and thousands of miles,
   From the Cape of Good Hope,
   Just to bugger the Pope,
But he couldn't—the pontiff had piles.

There was an old abbess quite shocked
To find nuns where the candles were locked.
   Said the abbess, "You nuns
   Should behave more like guns
And never go off till you're cocked."

There was a young monk of Siberia
Who of frigging grew weary and wearier.
   At last, with a yell,
   He burst from his cell
And buggered the father superior.

      There was a young monk from Siberia
      Whose morals were very inferior.
         He did to a nun
         What he shouldn't have done,
      And now she's a mother superior.

Three lustful young ladies of Simms
Were blessed with such over-size quims,
   The bishop of their diocese
   Got elephantiasis,
For his life wasn't all singing hymns.

A medieval recluse named Sissions
Was alarmed by his nightly emissions.
  His cell-mate, a sod,
   Said, "Leave it to God."
And taught him some nifty positions.

There once was a Bishop of Treet
Who decided to be indiscreet,
  But after one round
  To his horror he found
You repeat, and repeat, and repeat.

A bishop whose see was Vermont
Used to jerk himself off in the font.
  The baptistry stank
  With an odor most rank,
And no one would sit up in front.

Said a Palestine pilgrim named Wadham:
"For religion I don't give a goddamn!
   I've frequently peed in
   The Garden of Eden,
And buggered my guide when in Sodom."

7

Animal Behavior

There was a young man of Adair
Who thought he would diddle a mare.
    He climbed up a ladder
    And jolly well had her,
With his backside a-wave in the air.

    There was a young gaucho named Bruno
    Who said: "Screwing is one thing I do know.
        A woman is fine,
        And a sheep is divine,
    But a llama is Numero Uno."

There once was a sacred baboon
That lived by the river Rangoon,
    And all of the women
    That came to go swimmin'
He'd bang by the light of the moon.

There was a young man from Bangor
Who was tired and said to his whore,
  "If you'll only roll over
  I'll get my dog Rover,
And you can have six inches more."

There once was a man of Belfast
Whose balls out of iron were cast.
  He'd managed somehow
  To bugger a sow,
Thus you get pig iron, at last.

There was a young man of Bengal
Who went to a fancy dress ball.
  Just for a stunt,
  He dressed up as a cunt
And was fucked by a dog in the hall.

A habit obscene and bizarre
Has taken ahold of papa:
   He brings home young camels
   And other odd mammals,
And gives them a go at mama.

     The Communist Party's Earl Browder
     Was fucking a girl in a howda.
       The elephant's trunk
       Somehow got in her cunt
     Which, they felt, made it terribly crowded.

There was a young man of Australia
Who went on a wild bacchanalia.
   He buggered a frog,
   Two mice, and a dog,
And a bishop in fullest regalia.

Said an old taxidermist in Burreil,
As he skillfully mounted a squirrel,
   "This excess of tail is
   Obstructive to phallus;
One's much better off with a girl."

There was an old man of the Cape
Who buggered a Barbary ape.
   The ape said: "You fool!
   You've got a square tool;
You've buggered my arse out of shape."

A fisherman off of Cape Cod
Said, "I'll bugger that tuna, by God!"
   But the high-minded fish
   Resented his wish,
And nimbly swam off with his rod.

There once was a man of Cape Nod
Who attempted to bugger a cod
   When up came some scallops
   And nibbled his bollocks,
And now he's a eunuch, by God.

      Minnehaha was washing her clothes,
      Unexpectant of sorrows or woes.
         A snake, a sidewinder,
         Crawled in her behinder,
      Wiggled 'round and came out of her nose.

A sailor indulged in coitus
With a cow of the genus of Cetus.
   Piscatologists thundered,
   Biologists wondered,
At the anchor tattooed on the foetus.

A man who was richer than Croesus
Enjoyed being sucked off by feices,
    Till a vicious old hound
    Thought his stake was ground round,
And chewed it completely to pieces.

There once was a fairy named Cyril
Who was had in a wood by a squirrel,
    And he liked it so good
    That he stayed in the wood,
Just as long as the squirrel was virile.

There once was a clergyman's daughter
Who detested the pony he'd bought her
    Till she found that its dong
    Was as hard and as long
As the prayers her father had taught her.

She married a fellow named Tony
Who soon found her fucking the pony
   Said he, "What's it got,
   My dear, that I've not?"
Sighed she, "Just a yard-long bologna."

      That Harvard don down at El Djim—
      Oh, wasn't it nasty of him,
         With the whole harem randy,
         The sheik himself handy,
      To muss up a young camel's quim?

The eminent Mrs. DeVue
Was born in a cage at the zoo,
   And the curious rape
   Which made her an ape
Is highly fantastic, if true.

There was a young girl of Dundee
Who was raped by an ape in a tree.
    The result was most horrid—
    All ass and no forehead,
Three balls and a purple goatee.

Pine insulensis inevit
Rectum simioli quem scivit
    Proles infrontata
    Horrida glandata
Et semper violare cupivit.

The prior of Dunstan St. Just,
Consumed with erotical lust,
    Raped the bishop's prize fowls,
    Buggered four startled owls
And a little green lizard, that bust.

There was a young girl of Eau Claire
Who once was attacked by a bear.
   While chased in a field,
   She tripped and revealed
Some meat to the bear that was rare.

      There was a young man of Eau Claire
      Who had an affair with a bear,
         But the surly old brute
         With a snap of her snoot
      Left him only one ball and some hair.

When Theocritus guarded his flock,
He piped in the shade of a rock.
   It is said that his Muse
   Was one of the ewes
With a bum like a pink hollyhock.

There was a young lady named Florence
Who for fucking professed an abhorrence,
    But they found her in bed
    With her cunt flaming red,
And her poodle dog spending in torrents.

There once was a fellow named Fogg
Who attempted to bugger a hog.
    While engaged in his frolics
    The hog ate his bollocks,
And now he's a eunuch, by God.

One morning Mahatma Gandhi
Had a hard-on, and it was a dandy.
    So he said to his aide,
    "Please bring me a maid,
Or a goat, or whatever is handy."

There once was a man of Geneva
Who buggered a black bitch retriever.
   The result was a sow,
   Two horses, a cow,
Three lambs, and a London coal-heaver.

      There was a young peasant named Gorse
      Who fell madly in love with his horse.
         Said his wife, "You rapscallion,
         That horse is a stallion—
      This constitutes grounds for divorce."

There was an old man from near here,
Got awfully drunk upon beer.
   He fell in a ditch
   And a son of a bitch
Of a bulldog fucked him in the ear.

The Mahatma on Mt. Himavat
Opined as he diddled a cat,
  "She's a far better piece
  Than the viceroy's niece,
Who has also more fur on her prat."

A fox-hound retired from the hunt
For he found that his lobes had grown blunt
  To the scent of the fox,
  But he still would sniff rocks
For the mystical fragrance of cunt.

There was a young man with the itch
Who, because he was not at all rich,
  Had to harbor his tail
  In any female—
A duck or a sow or a bitch.

There was a young fellow named Jim
Whose wife kept a worm in her quim.
    It was silly and smelly,
    And tickled her belly,
And what the hell was it to him?

        A spinster in Kalamazoo
        Once strolled after dark by the zoo.
           She was seized by the nape
           And raped by an ape,
        And she murmured, "A wonderful screw."

And she added, "You're rough, yes, and hairy,
But I hope—yes I do—that I marry
    A man with a prick
    Half as stiff and as thick
As the kind that you zookeepers carry."

All the lady-apes ran from King Kong
For his dong was unspeakably long.
    But a friendly giraffe
    Quaffed his yard and a half,
And ecstatically burst into song.

Said a lovely young lady named Lake,
Pervertedly fond of a snake,
    "If my good friend, the boa,
    Shoots spermatozoa,
What offsprings we'll leave in our wake!"

Another young lady would make
Advances to snake after snake.
    Though men she had met
    Got her diaphragm wet,
She wanted her glottis to shake.

In a meadow a man named Llewellyn
Had a dream he was bundling with Helen.
   When he woke he discovered
   A bull had him covered
With ballocks as big as a melon.

There was an old Scot named McTavish
Who attempted an anthropoid ravish.
   The object of rape
   Was the wrong sex of ape,
And the anthropoid ravished McTavish.

There was a young man, a Maltese,
Who could even screw horses with ease.
   He'd flout natural laws
   In this manner because
Of his dong, which hung down to his knees.

Thus spake an old Chinese mandarin,
"There's a subject I'd like to use candor in:
   The geese of Pekin
   Are so steeped in sin
They'd as soon let a man as a gander in."

Here's to old King Montezuma,
For fun he would bugger a puma.
   The puma in play
   Clawed both balls away—
How's that for animal humor?

There was a young lady of Mott
Who inserted a fly up her twat
   And pretended the buzz
   Was not what it was
But something she knew it was not.

There was a young lady named Myrtle
Who had an affair with a turtle.
    She had crabs, so they say,
    In a year and a day,
Which proves that the turtle was fertile.

There was a young man from Nantucket,
Took a pig in a thicket to fuck it.
    Said the pig: "Oh, I'm queer,
    Get away from my rear . . .
Come around to the front and I'll suck it."

There once was a laddie of Neep
Who demanded everything cheap.
    When he wanted to screw,
    There was nothing to do
But take out his passion on sheep.

There was a young man from New Haven
Who had an affair with a raven.
   He said with a grin
   As he wiped off his chin,
"Nevermore!"

There was a young man of Newminster Court,
Bugger'd a pig, but his prick was too short.
   Said the hog, "It's not nice,
   But pray take my advice:
Make tracks, or by the police you'll be caught."

An elderly pervert in Nice
Who was long past desire for a piece
   Would jack off his dogs,
   His cows, and his dogs,
But his parrot called in the police.

There was a young man named O'Rourke,
Heard babies were brought by the stork,
   So he went to the zoo
   And attempted to screw
One old bird—end result: didn't work.

      The notorious Duchess of Peels
      Saw a fisherman fishing for eels.
         Said she: "Would you mind?—
         Shove one up my behind.
      I am anxious to know how it feels."

There was a young man in Peru
Who had nothing whatever to do,
   So he flew to the garret
   And buggered the parrot,
And sent the result to the zoo.

A gruff anthropoid of Piltdown
Had a strange way of going to town.
   With maniacal howls
   He would bugger young owls,
And polish his balls on their down.

There was a young Nubian prince
Whose cock would make elephants wince.
   Once, while socking the sperm
   To a large pachyderm,
He slipped, and he's not been seen since.

There was an old hostler named Rains,
Possessed of more ballocks than brains.
   He stood on a stool
   To bugger a mule,
And got kicked in the balls for his pains.

There once was a girl named Miss Randall
Who kept a young bear cub to dandle.
   She said, "In a pinch
   This bear cub's six-inch
Is almost as good as a candle."

There was a young lady of Rhodes
Who sinned in unusual modes.
   At the height of her fame
   She abruptly became
The mother of four dozen toads.

There was a young man of St. John's
Who wanted to bugger the swans.
   But the loyal hall porter
   Said: "Pray take my daughter!
Them birds are reserved for the dons."

There was a young man of St. Paul
Whose prick was exceedingly small.
   He could bugger a bug
   At the edge of a rug,
And the bug hardly felt it at all.

A hermit who lived on St. Roque
Had a lily perfected to poke.
    He diddled the donkeys
    And meddled with monkeys,
And would have done worse, but it broke.

There was an old man of Santander
Who attempted to bugger a gander.
    But that virtuous bird
    Plugged its ass with a turd,
And refused to such low tastes to pander.

There was a young man from Toulouse
Who thought he would diddle a goose.
    He hunted and bunted
    To get the thing cunted,
But decided it wasn't no use.

There was an old person of Sark
Who buggered a pig in the dark.
 The swine, in surprise,
 Murmured, "God blast your eyes,
Do you take me for Boulton or Park?"

   There once was a sergeant named Schmitt
   Who wanted a crime to commit.
    He thought raping women
    Was a little too common,
   So he buggered an aged tomtit.

There was a young lady named Schneider
Who often kept trysts with a spider.
 She found a strange bliss
 In the hiss of her piss,
As it strained through the cobwebs inside her.

8

Excrement

When a woman in strapless attire,
Found her breasts working higher and higher.
   A guest, with great feeling,
    Exclaimed: "How appealing!
Do you mind if I piss in the fire?"

     There was a young lady named Ames
     Who would play at the jolliest games.
        She was great fun to lay
        For her rectum would play
     Obbligatos, and call you bad names.

A young lady who lived in Astoria
Took a fancy to Fletcher's Castoria.
    She partook of this drink
    With her ass in the sink—
Now I ask you: ain't that foresight for ya?

       The rajah of Afghanistan
       Imported a Birmingham can,
          Which he set as a throne
          On a great Buddha stone—
       But he crapped out-of-doors like a man.

Sir Reginald Barrington, Bart,
Went to the masked ball as a fart.
    He had painted his face
    Like a more private place,
And his voice made the dowagers start.

There was a young fellow named Bart
Who strained every shit through a fart.
    Each tip-tapered turd
    Was the very last word
In this deft and most intricate art.

There was a young man of Bhogat
The cheeks of whose ass were so fat
    That they had to be parted
    Whenever he farted,
And propped wide apart when he shat.

    A cabman who drove in Biarritz
    Once frightened a fare into fits.
        When reprov'd for a fart,
        He said, "God bless my heart,
    When I break wind I usually shits."

There was a young fellow named Brewster
Who said to his wife as he goosed her,
   "It used to be grand
   But just look at my hand;
You ain't wiping as clean as you used to."

A nasty young joker named Bruce
Used to greet all his friends with a goose,
   Till it came to a stop
   In a handful of flop
From some bowels that were terribly loose.

There was a fat lady of Bryde
Whose shoelaces once came untied.
   She didn't dare stoop
   For fear she would poop,
And she cried and she cried and she cried.

There was a young man of Bulgaria
Who once went to piss down an area.
   Said Mary to cook:
   "Oh, do come and look.
Did you ever see anything hairier?"

There was a young friar of Byhill
Who went up to shit on a high hill.
   When the abbot asked, "Was it
   A goodly deposit?"
He said, "Vox et praeterea nihil."

There was an old Bey of Calcutta
Who greased up his asshole with butter.
   Instead of the roar
   Which came there before,
Came a soft, oleaginous mutter.

There once was a horse from Cape Verdes
Who produced most unusual turds
   By the simplest means:
   He'd eat corn and beans
And make succotash for the birds.

     A tourist who stopped at Capri
     Was had by an old maid for tea.
       When she wiggled, he said,
       As he patted her head,
     "Ah, you're changing the 't' to a 'p'!"

There was a young man named Cattell
Who knew psychophysics so well
   That each time he shit
   He'd stop, measure it—
Its length, and its breadth, and its smell.

An efficient young fellow named Cave
Said, "Think of the time that I save
　　By avoiding vacations
　　And sexy relations,
And taking a crap while I shave."

There was a young fellow named Charted
Who rubbed soap on his bung when it smarted,
　　And to his surprise
　　He received a grand prize
For the bubbles he blew when he farted.

A nasty old bugger of Cheltenham
Once shit in his bags as he knelt in 'em,
　　So he sold 'em at Ware
　　To a gentleman there
Who didn't much like what he smelt in 'em.

There was a young fellow of Chiselhurst
Who never could piss till he'd whistle first.
    One evening in June
    He lost track of the tune—
Dum-da-de-dee . . . and his bladder burst!

                There was a young fellow named Chivy
                Who, whenever he went to the privy,
                    First solaced his mind,
                    And then wiped his behind
                With some well-chosen pages of Livy.

Said the Duke to the Duchess of Chypre,
"Now, can paper's grand for a wiper,
    But I don't give a damn for
    This new-fangled camphor-
and-menthol impregnated paper."

Said the Duchess, "Well yes, I daresay
Plain bum-wad's all right in its way,
   But there's nothing so grand
   As some leaves, or you hand,
When you're out in the woods for a day."

A young bio-chemist named Dan
Always followed his nose to the can.
   He judged people best
   By the urinal test,
As to race and to sex and to clan.

There was a faith healer of Deal
Who said, "Although pain isn't real
   When, frightened by chance,
   I unload in my pants,
I dislike what I fancy I feel."

There was an old person of Delhi
Awoke with a pain in his belly,
    And to cure it, 'tis said,
    He shit in his bed,
And the sheets were uncommonly smelly.

    There was a young lady of Dexter
    Whose husband exceedingly vexed her,
        For whenever they'd start,
        He'd unfailingly fart
    With a blast that damn nearly unsexed her.

There was a young lady of Dorset
Who went to an underground closet.
    She screwed up her ass
    But passed only some gas,
And that wasn't tuppence-worth, was it?

There was a young woman named Dottie
Who said as she sat on her potty,
   "It isn't polite
   To do this in sight,
But then, who am I to be snotty?"

My neighbors, the dirty Miss Drews,
Stand on their doorstep and use,
   And tie up their tresses
   While the dogs make their messes,
And I am wiping my shoes.

There was a young fellow of Ealing,
Devoid of all delicate feeling
   When he read on the door:
   "Don't shit on the floor,"
He jumped up and shat on the ceiling.

The Marquesa de Excusador
Used to pee on the drawing room floor,
 For the can was so cold,
 And when one grows old,
To be much alone is a bore.

While watching some tragical farces,
The audience had a catharsis.
 Instead of real tears
 They wept with their rears,
Which proves that catharsis my arse is.

There was a young lady of Fismes
Who amazingly voided four streams.
 A friend poked around
 And a fly button found
Wedged tightly in one of her seams.

There was a young lady from France,
Supposed to play at a dance,
   She ate a banana
   And played the piano,
And music came out of her pants.

There was a young lady of Ghat
Who, never could sit but she shat.
   Oh, the seat of her drawers
   Was a chamber of horrors,
And they felt even fouler than that!

There once was a fellow named Glantz
Who, on entering a toilet in France,
   Was in such a heat
   To paper the seat,
He shit right into his pants.

Alas for a preacher named Hoke,
Whose shit was all stuck in his poke.
   He farted a blast
   That left hearers aghast,
But nothing emerged but some smoke.

A professor who taught at Holyoke
Had a bung like a red artichoke.
   She was greatly annoyed
   That each ripe hemorrhoid
Always quivered whenever she spoke.

There once was a builder named Howell
Who had a remarkable bowel.
   He built him a building
   Of brickwork and gilding
Using—what do you think—on his trowel.

That illustrious author, Dean Howells,
Had a terrible time with his bowels.
   His wife, so they say,
   Cleaned them out every day
With special elongated trowels.

Here's to the state of Iowa
Whose soil is soft and rich.
   We need no turd
   From your beautiful bird,
You red-headed son of a bitch.

There was a young man from Kilbryde
Who fell in a shit house and died.
   His heart-broken brother
   Fell into another,
And now they're interred side by side.

There was a young girl of La Plata
Who was widely renowned as a farter.
    Her defeaning reports
    At the Argentine sports
Made her much in demand as a starter.

Q. Flaccus in his third liber:
"The Romans have no wood-pulp fiber.
    A crapulent quorum
    Will squat in the Forum
And heave dirty stones in the Tiber."

There was a young man of Loch Leven
Who went for a walk about seven.
    He fell into a pit
    That was brimful of shit,
And now the poor bugger's in heaven.

An old G. I. custom long-rooted
Is to entering fledglings well-suited.
   In every latrine
   A bright sign is seen:
"Stand close, the next guy may be barefooted."

There was a young Georgian named Lynd
Who'd never in all his life sinned,
   For whenever he'd start
   He'd be jarred by a fart,
And his semen was gone with the wind.

There was a young man named McBride
Who could fart whenever he tried.
   In a contest he blew
   Two thousand and two,
And then shit and was disqualified.

There was a young man named McFee
Who was stung in the balls by a bee.
   He made oodles of money
   By oozing pure honey
Every time he attempted to pee.

        There was a young girl of Machias
        Whose bloomers were cut on the bias,
           With an opening behind
           To let out the wind,
        And to let the boys in once or twias.

There was a young fellow named Malcolm
Who dusted his asshole with talcum.
   He'd always use it
   Every time that he shit,
And found the sensation right welcome.

There was an old man of Madrid
Who went to an auction to bid.
   In the first lot they sold
    Was an ancient commode—
And, my god, when they lifted the lid!

There was a young Royal Marine
Who tried to fart "God Save the Queen."
   When he reached the soprano
   Out came the guano,
And his breeches weren't fit to be seen.

There is a professor named Martin
From whom I'm about to be partin',
   And on my way out
   He may hear me shout,
"It's your face I'd sure like to fart in."

9

Gourmands

There was a young Sapphic named Anna
Who stuffed her friend's cunt with banana,
  Which she sucked bit by bit
  From her partner's warm slit,
In the most approved lesbian manner.

There was a young girl of Antietam
Who liked horse turds so well she could eat 'em.
  She'd lie on their rumps
  And swallow the lumps
As fast as the beasts could excrete 'em.

There was a young man had the art
Of making a capital tart
   With a handful of shit,
   Some snot, and a spit,
And he'd flavor the whole with a fart.

There once was a midget named Carr
Who couldn't reach up to the bar,
   So in every saloon
   He climbed a spittoon,
And guzzled his liquor from thar.

There was a young man from the coast
Who ate melted shit on his toast.
   When the toast saw the shit,
   It collapsed in a fit,
For the shit was its grandfather's ghost.

There was an old man of Corfu
Who fed upon cunt juice and spew.
   When he couldn't get that,
    He ate what he shat—
And bloody good shit he shat, too.

On clinkers his choice often fell,
Or clabbered piss brought to a jell.
   When these palled to his taste,
    He tried snot and turd paste,
And found them delicious as well.

He ate them, and sighed, and said: "What
Uncommonly fine shit and snot!
   Now really, the two
    Are too good to be true—
I would rather have et them than not."

A Dutchman who dwelt in Dundee
Walked in to a grocer's named Lee.
   He said, "If you please,
   Haff you any prick cheese?"
Said the grocer, "I'll skin back and see."

    A coprophagous fellow named Fleam
    Loved to drink a strong urinal stream.
      He seduced little gonsils
      Into spraying his tonsils
    With the stuff he liked best on earth: cream.

There was a young fellow named Fritz
Who planted an acre of tits.
   They came up in the fall,
   Pink nipples and all,
And he chewed them all up into bits.

There was a young man of Glengarridge,
The fruit of a scrofulous marriage.
   He sucked off his brother
   And buggered his mother,
And ate up his sister's miscarriage.

A daughter of fair Ioway,
While at sport in the toilet one day,
   Swallowed some of her pee,
   "And hereafter," said she,
"I'll do it at lunch every day."

A young lady who once had a Jew beau
Found out soon that he'd got a bubo,
   So when it was ripe
   She put in a pipe,
And sucked up the juice through a tube oh!

There was a young fellow of Kent
Who had a peculiar bent.
   He collected the turds
   Of various birds,
And had them for lunch during Lent.

There was a young man of King's Cross
Who amused himself frigging a horse,
   Then licking the spend
   Which still dripped from the end,
Said, "It tastes just like anchovy sauce."

A hypocritical bastard named Legman
When drinking piss highballs puts egg in 'em.
   If he tells you you're queer
   To enjoy pissless beer,
Just say to him, "Quit pulling my leg, man!"

There was a young fellow from Leith
Who used to skin cocks with his teeth.
   It wasn't for pleasure
   He adopted this measure,
But to get at the cheese underneath.

Said a busy young whore known as Mable,
Who at fucking was willing and able,
   "It's a pity to waste
   All that juicy white paste,"
So she served it in bowls at the table.

There once was a U.S. marine
Whose manners were slightly obscene.
   He loved to eat jizz,
   Both others' and his,
When served in a hot soup tureen.

There was a young man from Marseilles
Who lived on clap juice and snails.
When tired of these,
He lived upon cheese
From his prick, which he picked with his nails.

There was an old maid from Shalot
Who lived upon frog shit and snot.
When she tired of these,
She would eat the green cheese
That she scraped from the sides of her twat.

There was an old sailor named Jock
Who was wrecked on a desolate rock.
He had nothing to eat
But the punk of his feet,
And the cheese from the end of his cock.

There once was a baker of Nottingham
Who in making éclairs would put snot in 'em.
    When he ran out of snot,
    He would, like as not,
Take his pecker and jack off a shot in 'em.

There was a young fellow of Perth,
The nastiest bastard on earth,
    When his wife was confined,
    He pulled down the blind,
And ate up the whole afterbirth.

A mannerly fellow named Phyfe
Was greatly distressed by his wife,
    For whene'er she was able,
    She'd shit on the table,
And gobble the shit—with her knife!

There were two little mice in Rangoon
Who sought lunch in an old lady's womb.
    Cried one mouse, "By Jesus,
    I'll wager this cheese is
As old as the cheese in the moon!"

    Where was a young lady of Rheims
    Who was terribly plagued with wet dreams.
      She saved up a dozen
      And sent to her cousin,
    Who ate them and thought they were creams.

An elderly rabbi named Riskin
Dines daily on cunt juice and foreskin.
    And to further his bliss,
    At dessert he'll drink piss,
For which he is always a-thirstin'.

There was a young man known as Royce
Who took an emetic by choice.
   He was fed, quite by chance,
   Half the crotch of the pants
Of a girl who kept crab lice as toys.

There was a young man of St. Just
Who ate of new bread till he bust.
   It was not the crumb,
   For that passed through his bum,
But what buggered him up was the crust.

10

Virginity

There was a young lady of Andover,
And the boys used to ask her to hand over
   Her sexual favor,
   Which she did (may God save her!)
For her morals she had no command over.

     "Competition is keen, you'll agree,"
     Said an ancient old flapper from Dee,
       So she dyed her gray tresses,
       Chopped a foot from her dresses,
     And her reason you plainly can see.

The bride went up the aisle
In traditional virginal style,
　　But they say she was nary
　　An innocent cherry,
But a whore from the banks of the Nile.

　　　　　There was a young virgin named Alice
　　　　　Who thought of her cunt as a chalice.
　　　　　　　One night, sleeping nude,
　　　　　　　She awoke feeling lewd,
　　　　　And found in her chalice a phallus.

A maiden sat under a tree
And played with the lad's fiddle-dee,
　　His little wood post—
　　Soon her jewel is lost
From the casket where it used to be.

There was a young girl named Anheuser
Who said that no man could surprise her,
　　But Pabst took a chance,
　　Found Schlitz in her pants,
And now she is sadder Budweiser.

To the shrine which was Pallas Athena's
Young Bito (who'd learned about penis)
　　Brought her needles and thread
　　And scissors and said,
"You can stick them—I'm changing to Venus!"

There's a tiresome young girl in Bay Shore,
When her fiancé cried, "I adore
　　Your beautiful twat!"
　　She replied, "Like as not—
It's pretty, but what is it for?"

There once was a tart named Belinda
Whose cunt opened out like a window.
   But she'd slam the thing shut,
   The contemptible slut,
Whenever you tried to get inda.

        A lisping young lady named Beth
        Was saved from a fate worse than death
           Seven times in a row,
           Which unsettled her so
        That she quit saying "No" and said "Yeth."

There was a young lady of Bhore
Who was courted by gallants galore.
   Their ardent protestin'
   She found interestin',
And ended her life as a virgin.

There was a young fellow named Biddle
Whose girl had to teach him to fiddle.
   She grabbed hold of his bow
   And said, "If you want to know,
You can try parting my hair in the middle."

In Stokes lived an ugly bluestocking
Who declared the men's manners were shocking.
   Why, she'd never been diddled,
   Even fingered or fiddled . . .
So she finally moved over to Focking.

There was a young virgin of Bude
Whose tricks, though exciting, were viewed
   With distrust by the males
   For she'd fondle their rails
But never would let them intrude.

There was an old spinster named Campbell,
Got tangled one day in a bramble.
   She cried: "Ouch, how it sticks!
   But so many sharp pricks
Are not met every day on a ramble."

There was a young girl from the Cape
Who filled her hole with bicycle tape
   To ease up the pangs
   Caused by the whangs
Of gentlemen bent upon rape.

There was a young miss from Cape Cod
Who at soldiers would not even nod.
   But she tripped in a ditch
   And some son of a bitch
Of a corporal raped her, by God!

There once was a passionate Celt
Who'd an urge to know how a cock felt.
   One went in, hard and straight,
   But her heat was so great
That she found she had caused it to melt.

A Salvation lassie named Claire
Was having her first love affair.
   As she climbed into bed
   She reverently said,
"I wish to be opened with prayer."

An innocent maiden of Clewer
Incited her boyfriend to screw her.
   She tried to say no,
   A half second slow—
Now when she sits down she says, "Oo-er!"

There was a young lady of Corbie
Who said: "Oh, the men really bore me!
    But I reckon, without 'em,
     Though I hate 'em and scout 'em,
There just would be no one to scour me."

        There was a young lady of Crewe
        Whose cherry a chap had got through,
          Which she told to her mother,
          Who fixed her another
        Out of rubber and red ink and glue.

There was a young princess called Dagmar
Who said, "I should so like to shag, Ma,"
    And says she, "If you speaks
     To the king of the Greeks,
He will lend me his own tolliwag, Ma."

There was a young girl of Dalkeith
With a hymen in need of relief,
    So she went to the doctor
    Who prodded and shocked her,
And stretched it with fingers and teeth.

A girl named Alice, in Dallas,
Had never felt of a phallus.
    She remained virgo intacto,
    Because, ipso facto,
No phallus in Dallas fit Alice.

An ignorant virgin of Dee
Entertained a man's cock just to see
    If the darn thing would fit—
    It went off in her pit,
And she cried: "Hey! That's no place to pee!"

A young lady who taught at Devizes
Was had up at the local assizes
   For teaching young boys
   Matrimonial joys,
And giving French letters as prizes.

     A complacent old don of Divinity
     Made boast of his daughter's virginity.
        They must have been dawdlin'
        Down at old Magdalen—
     It couldn't have happened at Trinity.

There was a young virgin of Dover
Who was raped in the woods by a drover.
   When the going got hard,
   He greased her with lard,
Which felt nice, so they started all over.

There was a young girl of East Lynne
Whose mother, to save her from sin,
    Had filled up her crack
    To the brim with shellac,
But the boys picked it out with a pin.

The first love of a lady named Ederle
Found her hymen obstructed him steadily,
    But he merely rubbed lard on
    The end of his hard-on,
And then found he entered quite readily.

There was a bluestocking in Florence
Wrote anti-sex pamphlets in torrents,
    Till a Spanish grandee
    Got her off with his knee,
And she burned all her works with abhorrence.

A homely old spinster of France,
Who all the men looked at askance,
   Threw her skirt overhead
   And then jumped into bed,
Saying, "Now I've at least half a chance."

        There was a young fellow named Fyfe
        Who married the pride of his life,
           But imagine his pain
           When he struggled in vain,
        And just couldn't get into his wife.

A neuropath virgin named Flynn
Shouted before she gave in,
   "It isn't the deed,
   Or the fear of the seed,
But that big worm that's shedding its skin!"

There was a young fellow named Gluck
Who found himself shit out of luck.
    Though he petted and wooed,
    When he tried to get screwed
He found virgins just don't give a fuck.

There was an old spinster named Gretel
Who wore underclothes made of metal.
    When they said, "Does it hurt?"
    She said, "It keeps dirt
From stamen and pistil and petal."

There were three young ladies of Grimsby
Who said: "Of what use can our quims be?
    The hole in the middle
    Is so we can piddle,
But for what can the hole in the rims be?"

There was a young lady of Harwich
Who said on the morn of her marriage,
   "I shall sew my chemise
   Right down to my knees,
For I'm damned if I fuck in the carriage!"

I don't mind if a girl rides a hel'copter,
I don't mind if a girl rides a car,
   But the girl who rides straddle
   An old-fashioned saddle
Is stretching things a bit too far.

There was a young girl from Hoboken
Who claimed that her hymen was broken
   From riding a bike
   On a cobblestone pike,
But it really was broken from pokin'.

There was a young brave who got hot
And chased an old squaw who was not.
   So she stuffed her canal
   With some dried chaparral,
And sprinkled some sand on her twat.

A lady of virginal humours
Would only be screwed through her bloomers.
   But one fatal day
   The bloomers gave way,
Which fixed her for future consumers.

A girl who lived in Kentucky
Said: "Yes, I've been awfully lucky.
   No man ever yet
   On my back made me get,
But sometimes I feel awful fucky."

Exclaimed a young girl in Kildare,
As her lover's jock towered in air,
　　"If that goes in me, I
　　Shall certainly die—
As I shall if it does not go there."

　　　　There was an old lady of Leicester,
　　　　And no man had ever caressed her,
　　　　　　And all day she'd wriggle
　　　　　　And giggle and jiggle,
　　　　As though seven devils possessed her.

A coon who was out with his Liz
Said, "Baby, let's get down to biz."
　　Said she, "That cain't be,
　　'Less you'se stronger'n me,
But, honey, I reckon you is."

There was a young girl named McKnight
Who got drunk with her boyfriend one night.
   She came to in bed
   With a split maidenhead—
That's the last time she ever was tight.

That Jew girl, the famed Virgin Mary,
Said: "Oh God, my quim's got all hairy!
   To hell with virginity,
   I'll fuck the whole Trinity!
I'm tired of vice solitary."

No one can tell about Myrtle
Whether she's sterile or fertile.
   If anyone tries
   To tickle her thighs,
She closes them tight like a turtle.

There was a young widow of Nain
Who the bedclothes did frequently stain—
   With such great inflammation
   Came such menstruation,
Her cunt so long idle had lain.

      A certain young sheik I'm not namin'
      Asked a flapper he thought he was tamin',
         "Have you your maidenhead?"
         "Don't be foolish," she said,
      "But I still have the box that it came in."

There is a young girl from New York
Who is cautious from fear of the stork.
   You will find she is taped
   To prevent being raped,
And her asshole is plugged with a cork.

There was a young girl of Ostend
Who her maidenhead tried to defend,
But a Chasseur d'Afrique
Inserted his prick
And taught that ex-maid how to spend.

There was a young fellow from Oudh
Whose mind was excessively lewd.
He asserted, "All women
Seen dancin' or swimmin'
Would rather be home gettin' screwed."

A girl at whom no one made passes
No longer resents wearing glasses,
For two FBI men
Demolished her hymen
On failing to find her *New Masses*.

There was a young virgin in Perth,
Swore she'd do it for no one on earth,
   Yet she fell without scandal
   To a red Christmas candle
And was always less choosy henceforth.

There was an old maid in Peru
Who'd a dog and a cat and a gnu.
   From a sailor named Harrot
   She bought an old parrot,
And he threw in a young cockatoo.

There was a young lassie named Phyllis,
Was deflowered one night in a Willys.
   Before they were through,
   Her spine was askew,
And I very much fear that it still is.

A Newfoundland lad from Placentia
Was in love to the point of dementia,
   But his love couldn't burgeon
   With his touch-me-not virgin
'Til he screwed her by hand in absentia.

There was a young lady from 'Quoddie
Who had a magnificent body,
   And her face was not bad,
   Yet she'd never been had,
For her odor was markedly coddy.

A pathetic appellant at Reno
Was as chaste as the holy Bambino,
   For she'd married a slicker
   Who stuck to his liquor
And scorned her ripe maraschino.

There was a young man of St. Kitt
Who was screwing a spinster, but quit.
    Said she, "Don't be scary,
    It's only my cherry,"
But he said, "It feels more like a pit."

        There was a young girl of Samoa
        Who determined that no man should know her.
           One young fellow tried,
           But she wriggled aside,
        And spilled all the spermatozoa.

Maggie is such a sad sack of shit
That no one will tickle her tit.
    It would make her so glad
    To be had by a lad,
Her drawers cream at the mere thought of it.

There was a young fellow named Simon
Who tried to discover a hymen,
   But he found every girl
   Had relinquished her pearl
In exchange for a solitaire diamond.

There was a T/5, name of Snyder,
Who took out a girl just to ride her.
   She allowed him to feel
   From her neck to her heel,
But never would let him inside her.

There was a young girl from Sofia
Who succumbed to her lover's desire.
   She said, "It's a sin,
   But now that it's in,
Could you shove it a few inches higher?"

There was a young girl of Spitzbergen
Whose people all thought her a virgin,
    Till they found her in bed
    With her quim very red,
And the head of a kid just emergin'.

An innocent soldier named Stave
Was almost seduced by a Wave,
    But he's still a recluse
    With all of his juice,
For he didn't know how to behave.

There was a young fellow named Sweeney
Whose girl was a terrible meanie.
    The hatch of her snatch
    Had a catch that would latch—
She could only be screwed by Houdini.

A proper young lady of Taos
Had her panties trimmed neatly with lace,
    But a vulgar young man
    Raped her roughly, and ran,
And left them pure panties in chaos.

11

Motherhood

There was a young girl who begat
Three brats, by name Nat, Pat, and Tat.
   It was fun in the breeding
   But hell in the feeding,
When she found there was no tit for Tat.

A young PhD passing by,
She gave him the problem to try.
   He worked the division
   With perfect precision,
And the answer was B-A-B-Y.

To a widow bereaved of Barrientos,
Her marital divertimentos
  Are so sentimental—
  Even things contraceptal,
That old fishkins are dearest mementos.

There once was a Vassar B.A.
Who pondered the problem all day
  Of what there would be
  If C-U-N-T
Were divided by C-O-C-K.

There was a young girl of Bombay
Who was put in the family way
  By the mate of a lugger,
  An ignorant bugger
Who always spelled "cunt" with a "k."

An indolent vicar of Bray
Kept his wife in the family way,
   Till she grew more alert,
   Bought a vaginal squirt,
And said to her spouse, "Let us spray!"

There was a young man of Cape Cod
Who once put my wife into pod.
   His name, it was Tucker,
   The dirty old fucker,
The bugger, the blighter, the sod!

There was a young man of Cape Horn
Who wished he had never been born.
   And he wouldn't have been
   If his father had seen
That the end of the rubber was torn.

There was a young pessimist, Grotton,
Who wished he had ne'er been begotten,
    Nor would he have been,
    But the rubber was thin,
And right at the tip it was rotten.

        There once was a modern young chick
        Who wished above all to be chic.
            She thought it much neater
            (Not to mention discreeter)
        To do it with a sheik with a "Sheik."

There was a young girl of Claridge's
Who said, "What a strange thing marriage is,
    When you stop to think
    That I've poured down the sink
Five abortions and fifty miscarriages!"

There was an old lady, God damn her,
She fucked herself with a hammer.
   The hammer was blunt,
    And so was her cunt,
And out came a kid with a hop, skip, and jump.

There was a young lady of Delhi
Who had a bad pain in her belly.
   Her relations all smiled
    'Cause they found her with child
By his honour, the chief batsman Kelly.

There was a young girl whose divinity
Preserved her in perfect virginity,
   'Til a candle, her nemesis,
    Caused parthenogenesis—
Now she thinks herself one of the Trinity.

A pious young lady named Finnegan
Would caution her beau, "Now you're in again,
   Please watch it just right
   So you'll last through the night,
For I certainly don't want to sin again."

       There was a young girl from the five-and-ten
       Who diddled herself with a fountain pen.
         The top came off,
         The ink went wild,
       And now she's the mother of a colored child.

There was a young lady named Flo
Whose lover had pulled out too slow.
   So they tried it all night
   Till he got it just right. . .
Well, practice makes pregnant, you know.

There was a young lady of France
Who went to the palace to dance.
    She danced with a Turk
    Till he got in his dirk,
And now she can't button her pants.

There once was a midwife of Gaul
Who had hardly no business at all.
    She cried: "Hell and damnation!
    There's no procreation—
God made the French penis too small."

My wife Myrtle's womb has a habit
Of expanding whenever I stab it.
    What's more, my wife Myrtle
    Is so wondrously fertile
That she's giving me kids like a rabbit.

There once was a handsome Haitian,
The luckiest dog in creation.
    He worked for the rubber trust,
     Teaching the upper crust
The science of safe copulation.

        There was a young lady named Hall
        Who went to a birth control ball.
          She was loaded with pessaries
          And other accessories,
        But no one approached her at all.

A medical student named Hetrick
Is learned in matters obstetric.
    From a glance at the toes
    Of the mother, he knows
If the fetus's balls are symmetric.

Old King Cole was a bugger for the hole,
And a bugger for the hole was he.
  He called for his wife
  And stuck her with a knife,
And out jumped a K-I-D.

There was a young man of Jesus
Who performed cheap abortions with tweezers.
  One night, in a hunt
  Up a mummified cunt,
He found a French letter of Caesar's.

There was a young lady of Louth
Who suddenly grew very stout.
  Her mother said, "Nelly,
  There's more in your belly
Than ever went in through your mouth."

There was a young lady from Thrace
Whose corsets got too tight to lace.
　　Her mother said, "Nelly,
　　There's things in your belly
That never got in through your face."

　　　Frankie and Johnny were lovers,
　　　Especially under the covers.
　　　　When she pulled out his trigger,
　　　　She said, "Mmm, what a figger!
　　　But it makes so many girls mothers."

There was a young girl of Madrid
Who thought she'd be having a kid.
　　So by holding her water
　　Three months and a quarter
She drowned the poor bastard, she did.

There once was an Indian maid,
A whore she was by trade—
    For two-bits a whack
    She'd lay on her back,
And let the cowboys ram it up her crack.

There was a young lady of Maine
Who declared she'd a man on the brain.
    But you knew from the view
    Of the way her waist grew,
It was not on her brain that he'd lain.

There was an old whore of Marseilles
Who tried the new rotary spray.
    Said she: "Ah, that's better . . .
    Why, here's a French letter
That's been missing since Armistice Day!"

A lazy young lady named May
Was a torrid but troublesome lay.
   She was prone to conceive,
   So made haste to achieve
A bed with a built-in bidet.

        Said a girl to her friend from Milpitas,
        "There's a doctor in town who will treat us
           For feminine ills
           And hot and cold chills,
        Or even abort a young foetus."

There once was an innocent miss
Who feared she'd conceived from a kiss.
   So, as a precaution,
   She had an abortion,
But naught was forthcoming but piss.

There was a young girl from New York
Who expected a call from the stork.
    So with infinite caution
    She performed an abortion
With an ice pick, a spoon, and a fork.

There was a young man, Mussolini,
Who found he had seven bambini.
    He said, "If I thought
    That the griddle was hot,
I'd never have put in the weenie!"

There was a young lady named Myrtle
Whose womb was exceedingly fertile.
    Her pa got contortions
    At all her abortions,
And bought her a chastity girdle.

Said a young man of Novorossisk:
"I use vulcanization by Fisk.
　　Of course it comes higher,
　　But when it's time to retire,
You can frisk with a minimal risk."

　　　　There was a young fellow named Oram,
　　　　A model of tact and decorum.
　　　　　　When about to fuck Grishkin,
　　　　　　He pulled out a fishskin
　　　　From the leaves of the Keats variorum.

There was a young man of Penzance
Who rogered his three maiden aunts.
　　Though them he defiled,
　　He ne'er got them with child,
Through using the letters of France.

There was a young girl from Penzance
Who decided to take just one chance.
   So she let herself go
   In the lap of her beau,
And now all her sisters are aunts.

In spring Miss May marries Perce.
'Til then their pash' they disburse :
   With a thin piece of rubber
   There's no need to scrub 'er—
Of course, there's no harm to rehearse.

There was a young fellow named Peter
Who was laying his gal with a cheater
   When the rubber thing broke
   And started to smoke
From the friction with her piss hole (ureter).

We've socially conscious biography,
Esthetics, and social geography.
    Today every field
    Boasts its Marxian yield,
So now there's class-conscious pornography.

A grey-headed tutor named Porson
From some strange amatory contortion
    Believed he'd conceived
    A book, but relieved
Himself by a pamphlet abortion.

Young girls of seductive proportions
Should take contraceptive precautions:
    Silly young Ermintrude
    Let one small sperm intrude . . .
Who's the best man for abortions?

A cautious young husband named Rafe
Used to diddle his wife with a safe.
    Thus he thwarted God's wishes
    And fed his pet fishes,
Which he kept in a bedside carafe.

12

Prostitution

There once was a girl from Alaska
Who would fuck whenever you'd ask her.
    But soon she grew nice
    And went up in price,
And no one could touch her but Jesus H. Christ,
Or possibly John Jacob Astor.

A vicious old whore of Albania
Hated men with a terrible mania.
    With a twitch and a squirm
    She would hold back your sperm,
And then roll on her face and disdain ya.

There was an old whore of Algiers
Who had bushels of dirt in her ears.
 The tip of her titty
 Was also quite shitty,
She never had washed it in years.

   A guy met a girl in Anacostia
   And said: "Darling, dare I accost ya?
    I got only a buck,
    Is that good for a fuck?"
   She replied, "Not a fart will it cost ya."

There once was a floozie named Annie
Whose prices were cosy—but canny:
 A buck for a fuck,
 Fifty cents for a suck,
And a dime for a feel of her fanny.

Said an elderly whore named Arlene:
"I prefer a young lad of eighteen.
    There's more cream in his larder,
    And his pecker gets harder,
And he fucks in a manner obscene."

When the Duchess of Bagliofuente
Took her fourteenth cavaliere servente,
    The Duke said, "Old chappy,
    I'll keep that quim happy
If I have to hire nineteen or twenty."

There was a young man from Berlin,
A patron of sexual sin,
    He crammed the small crease
    'Twixt the legs of his niece
With a foot of his old rolling pin.

There was a young chip from Brazil
Who fucked like a veritable mill.
　　There was never a whore,
　　When she'd finished her chore,
More prompt to present you her bill.

There was a young trucker named Briard
Who had a young whore that he hired
　　To fuck when not trucking,
　　But trucking plus fucking
Got him so fucking tired he got fired.

There was a young fellow called Cary,
Who got fucking the Virgin Mary.
　　And Christ was so bored
　　At seeing Ma whored
That he set himself up as a fairy.

There once was a girl from the chorus
Whose virtue was known to be porous.
    She started by candling,
    And ended by handling
The whole clientele of a whorehouse.

A hard-working waitress named Cora
Discovered that drummers adore a
    Titty that's ripe
    And a cunt that is tripe—
Now she doesn't work hard any more-a!

A lady named Belle da Cunt Corrigan
Was the mistress of J. Pierpont Morigan
    Till she handed the banker
    A hell of a chancre,
And now she is just a plain whore again.

There was a young harlot of Crete
Whose fucking was far, far too fleet.
   So they tied down her ass
   With a long ton of brass
To give them a much longer treat.

     When the Nazis landed in Crete,
     This young lady had to compete
        With the many Storm Troopers
        Who were using their poopers
     For other things than to excrete.

Our subversive young harlot of Crete
Was led to fifth column deceit.
   When the paratroops landed,
   Her trade she expanded
By at once going down on their meat.

Then here was this harlot of Crete,
She decided to be very neat.
  She said, "I'm too high class
  To ream common ass,
And I'll wash every prick that I eat."

And at last this fine harlot of Crete
Was hawking her meat in the street.
  Ambling out one fine day
  In a casual way,
She clapped up the whole British fleet.

There was a young lady from Cue
Who filled her vagina with glue.
  She said with a grin,
  "If they pay to get in,
They'll pay to get out of it too."

There was a young girl named Dale
Who put up her ass for sale.
   For the sum of two bits
   You could tickle her tits,
But a buck would get you real tail.

      To succeed in the brothels at Derna
      One always begins as a learner.
         Indentured at six
         As a greaser of pricks,
      One may rise to be fitter and turner.

There was a young girl from Des Moines
Who had a large sack full of coins.
   The nickels and dimes
   She got from the times
That she cradled the boys in her loins.

A passion-swept dame called Dolores
Is the hottest of history's whores.
    Though we fuck her with zest,
    When we crawl home to rest,
Guess who's there waiting for us—
Dolores, of cour-es!

A young man, quite free with his dong,
Said the thing could be had for a song.
    Such response did he get
    That he rented the Met,
And held auditions all the day long.

A sempstress at Epping-on-Tyne
Used to peddle her tail down the line.
    She first got a crown,
    But her prices went down—
Now she'll fit you for ten pence or nine.

There was a young lady of Erskine,
And the chief of her charms was her fair skin,
    But the sable she wore
    (She had several more)
She had earned while wearing her bare skin.

        Two young girls who lived in Ft. Tunney
        Decided to shop their dofunny.
           "We had papa tutor us
           To cash in on our uterus;
        We park transients now, in each cunny!"

Said the whore whom they called Geraldine,
"When I think of the pricks that I've seen,
    And all of the nuts
    And the assholes and butts,
And the bastards like you in between . . . "

A notorious whore named Miss Hearst
In the weakness of men is well versed.
   Reads a sign o'er the head
   Of her well-rumpled bed,
"The customer always comes first."

Said a pretty young whore of Hong Kong
To a long-pronged patron named Wong,
   "They say my vagina's
   The nicest in China—
Don't ruin it by donging it wrong."

There was a young man of Jaipur
Whose cock was shot off in the war.
   So he painted the front
   To resemble a cunt,
And set himself up as a whore.

Since donning a uniform, Joe
Quit the floozies that he used to know.
   Says he, "Joan Bennett'll
   Tickle my genital
Every night at the old U.S.O."

A shiftless young fellow of Kent
Had his wife fuck the landlord for rent.
   But as she grew older,
   The landlord grew colder,
And now they live out in a tent.

There was an old girl of Kilkenny
Whose usual charge was a penny.
   For the half of that sum
   You could finger her bum—
A source of amusement to many.

Said a madam named Mamie La Farge
To a sailor just off of a barge,
    "We have one girl that's dead,
    With a hole in her head—
Of course there's a slight extra charge."

Have you heard about Dorothy Lamour,
Whose lovers got fewer and fewer?
    When asked why she lost 'em,
    She said, "I defrost 'em—
I guess I'm not made for a whore."

In the city of York there's a lass
Who will hitch up her dress when you pass.
    If you toss her two bits,
    She will strip to the tits,
And let you explore her bare ass.

A harlot of note named Le Dux
Would always charge seventy bucks.
   But for that she would suck you,
   And wink off and fuck you—
The whole things was simply de luxe!

There was an old hag named Le Sueur
Who just was an out-and-out whore.
   Between her big teats
   You could come for two bits,
And she'd fuck in any old sewer.

Any whore whose door sports a red light
Knows a prick when she sees one, all right.
   She can tell by a glance
   At the drape of men's pants
If they're worth taking on for the night.

There was a young whore from Madrid
Who anyone could fuck for a quid.
    But a bastard Italian
    With balls like a stallion
Said he'd do it for nothing—and did.

There was a young lady named Mable
Who would fuck on a bed or a table.
    Though a two-dollar screw
    Was the best she could do,
Her ass bore a ten-dollar label.

Les cocottes de la ville de Marseille
Sont brunettes de l'ardent soleil.
    Elles pissent du vin blanc,
    Couchent pour dix francs—
Mais ou sont les patentes de santè?

The tarts in the town of Marseilles
Are brunette from the sun every day.
   White wine is their piddle,
    For ten francs they'll diddle—
But their tickets of health, where are they?

      Unique is a strumpet of Mazur
      In the way that her clientèle pays her.
        A machine that she uses
        Clamps on to her whoosis,
      And clocks everybody that lays her.

There was an old whore named McGee
Who was just the right sort for a spree.
   She said, "For a fuck I charge half a buck,
And I throw in the asshole for free."

Said a dainty young whore named Miss Meggs,
"The men like to spread my two legs,
　　Then slip in between,
　　If you know what I mean,
And leave me the white of their eggs."

Said a naked young soldier named Mickey
As his cunt eyed his stiff, throbbing dickey,
　　"Kid, my leave's almost up,
　　But I feel like a tup;
Bend down, and I'll slip you a quickie."

A schoolmarm from old Mississippi
Had a quim that was simply zippy.
　　The scholars all praised it
　　Till finally she raised it
To prices befitting a chippy.

There was a young thing from Missouri
Who fancied herself as a houri.
   Her friends thus forsook her,
   For a harlot they took her,
And she gave up the role in a fury.

There was a young lady named Moore
Who, while not quite precisely a whore,
   Couldn't pass up a chance
   To take down her pants
And compare some man's stroke with her bore.

A tired young trollop of Nome
Was worn out from her toes to her dome.
   Eight miners came screwing,
   But she said, "Nothing doing:
One of you has to go home!"

There was a young woman of Norway
Who drove a rare trade in the whore way,
　　Till a sodomite Viscount
　　Brought cunt to a discount
And the bawdy house belles to a poor way.

Said Clark Gable, picking his nose
"I get more than the public suppose.
　　Take the Hollywood way,
　　It's the women who pay,
And the men simply take off their clothes."

A chippy whose name was O'Dare
Sailed on a ship to Kenmare,
　　But this cute little honey
　　Had left home her money,
So she laid the whole crew for her fare.

A sailor ashore in Peru
Said, "Signora, quanto por la screw?"
 "For only one peso
  I will, if you say so,
Be buggered and nibble it too."

   A sprightly young tart in Pompeii
   Used to make fifty drachma per lay.
    But age dimmed her renown,
    And now she lies down
   Fifty times for the same pay.

A soi-disant Mynheer professor
Met a beat-up old whore from Odessa.
 She applied all her arts
 To his genital parts,
But they only grew lesser and lesser.

Says a busy young whore named Miss Randalls,
As men by the dozens she handles,
  "When I get this busy
  My cunt gets all jizzy,
And it runs down my legs like wax candles."

A whorehouse at 9 Rue de Rennes
Had trouble in luring in men,
  Till they got some fairies
  With pretty dillberries,
And their clientele came back again.

There was a young lady in Reno
Who lost all her dough playing keeno,
  But she lay on her back
  And opened her crack,
And now she owns the casino.

A prosperous merchant of Rhone
Took orders for cunt on the phone,
  Or the same could be baled,
  Stamped, labeled, and mailed
To a limited parcel post zone.

DuPont, I. G., Monsanto, and Shell
Built a world-circling pussy cartel,
  And by planned obsolescence
  So controlled detumescence
A poor man could not get a smell.

There was a rich old roué
Who felt himself slipping away.
  He endowed a large ward
  In a house where he'd whored.
Was there a crowd at his funeral? I'll say!

There was a hot girl from the Saar
Who fucked all, both from near and from far.
    When asked to explain,
    She replied with disdain,
"I'm trying to buy me a car."

There was a young girl from St. Cyr
Whose reflex reactions were queer:
    Her escort said, "Mable,
    Get up off the table;
That money's to pay for the beer."

A licentious old justice of Salem
Used to catch all the harlots and jail 'em,
    But instead of a fine,
    He would stand them in line,
With his common-law tool to impale 'em.

There was an old girl of Silesia
Who said, "As my cunt doesn't please ya,
   You might as well come
   Up my slimy old bum,
But be careful my tapeworm don't seize ya."

        Ethnologists up with the Sioux
        Wired home for two punts, one canoe.
           The answer next day
           Said, "Girls on the way,
        But what the hell's a 'panoe'?"

There was a young lady from Slough
Who said that she didn't know how.
   Then a young fellow caught her
   And jolly well taught her;
She lodges in Pimlico now.

Said a girl from Staraya Russa,
Whom the war had made looser and looser,
   "Yes, I'm wormin' a German,
   A vermin named Hermann,
But his dink is a lollapalooza!"

There was an old Count of Swoboda
Who would not pay a whore what he owed her.
   So with great savoir-faire
   She stood on a chair,
And pissed in his whiskey-and-soda.

There was an old man of Tagore
Who tried out his cook as a whore.
   He used Bridget's twidget
   To fidget his digit,
And now she won't cook any more.

There was a young whore from Tashkent
Who managed an immoral tent.
    Day out and day in
    She lay writhing in sin,
Giving thanks it was ten months to Lent.

A young girl who was no good at tennis,
But at swimming was really a menace,
    Took pains to explain,
    "It depends how you train:
I was a streetwalker in Venice."

There was a young man from the War Office
Who got into bed with a whore of his.
    She took off her drawers
    With many a pause,
But the chap from the War Office tore off his.

There was an old whore of Warsaw
Who fucked all her customers raw.
  She would thump with her rump,
  And punt with her cunt,
And lick every prick that she saw.

There once was a knowledgeful whore
Who knew all the coital lore.
  But she found there were many
  Who preferred her fat fanny,
And now she don't fuck anymore.

There once was a versatile whore,
As expert behind as before.
  For a quid you could view her,
  And bugger and screw her,
As she stood on her head on the floor.

13

Disease

Remember those two of Aberystwyth
Who connected the things that they pissed with?
   She sat on his lap
   But they both had the clap,
And they cursed with the things that they
kissed with.

A sultan named Abou ben Adhem
Thus cautioned a traveling madam,
   "I suffer from crabs
   As do most us A-rabs,"
"It's alright," said the madam, "I've had 'em."

There was an old whore of Azores
Whose cunt was all covered with sores.
   The dogs in the street
   Wouldn't eat the green meat
That hung in festoons from her drawers.

      There was a young fellow—a banker,
      Had bubo, itch, pox, and chancre.
         He got all the four
         From a dirty old whore,
      So he wrote her a letter to thank her.

There was a young man of Back Bay
Who thought syphilis just went away,
   And felt that a chancre
   Was merely a canker
Acquired in lascivious play.

There was a young girl of Bavaria
Who thought her disease was malaria.
  But the family doc
  Remarked to her shock,
"It is in the mercurial area."

A noble young lord named Bellasis
Was a sad case of satyriasis,
  Till help psychiatric
  Brought the fucking fanatic
To a state of sexual stasis.

There was a young man of Berlin
Whom disease had despoiled of his skin,
  But he said with much pride,
  "Though deprived of my hide,
I can still enjoy a put-in."

There was a young man of Cashmere
Who purchased a fine Bayadere.
   He fucked all her toes,
   Her mouth, eyes, and her nose,
And eventually poxed her left ear.

        There was a young woman of Cheadle
        Who once gave the clap to a beadle.
           Said she, "Does it itch?"
           "It does, you damned bitch,
        And burns like Hellfire when I peedle."

There was a young woman of Chester
Who said to the man who undressed her,
   "I think you will find
   That it's better behind—
The front is beginning to fester."

There was an old sarge of Dorchester
Who invented a mechanical whore tester.
   With an electrical eye,
   His tool, and a die,
He observed each sore, pimple, and fester.

There's a man in the city of Dublin
Whose pego is always him troubling,
   And it's now come to this,
   That he can't go to piss,
But the spunk with the piddle comes bubbling.

There was a young priest of Dundee
Who went back of the parish to pee.
   He said: "Pax vobiscum,
   Why doesn't the piss come?
I must have the C-L-A-P."

There was an old party of Fife
Who suspected a clap in his wife.
   So he bought an injection
   To cure the infection,
Which gave him a stricture for life.

There was a young rounder named Fisk
Whose method of screwing was brisk.
   And his reason was, "If
   The damned bitch has the syph,
This way I'm reducing the risk."

A horny young soldier named Frank
Had only his girlfriend to thank
   That he didn't catch clap,
   Gonorrhea, or pap,
And wind up in an oxygen tank.

A president called Gambetta
Once used an imperfect French letter.
   This was not the worst—
   With disease he got cursed,
And he took a long time to get better.

There was a young lady of Gaza
Who shaved her cunt clean with a razor.
   The crabs in a lump
   Made tracks to her rump,
Which proceeding did greatly amaze her.

There was an old man of Goditch,
Had the syph and the clap and the itch.
   His name was McNabs
   And he also had crabs,
The dirty old son of a bitch.

There was a young lady from Ipswich
Who had syphilis, pox, and the itch.
    In her box she put pepper
    And slept with a leper,
And ruined that son of a bitch.

A lecherous fellow named Gould
Soliloquized thus to his tool:
    "From Cape Cod to Salamanca,
    You've had pox, clap, and chancre—
Now ain't you a bloody great fool?"

There was a young lady of Grotton,
Had to plug up her coosie with cotton,
    For it was no myth
    That the girl had the syph—
She stunk, and her titties were rotten.

There was a young woman of Hadley
Who would with an omnibus cad lie.
   He gave her the crabs,
   And besides minor scabs,
The pox too she got very badly.

A strapping young fellow named Herman
Had a ring round his prick that was permanent.
   All the old docs
   Said the ring was the pox,
But he swore it was lipstick or vermin.

There was a young lady named Hitchin
Who was scratching her crotch in the kitchen.
   Her mother said, "Rose,
   It's the crabs, I suppose."
She said, "Yes, and the buggers are itchin'."

Young Tom Doane, a promising jockey,
Laid up his spurs, feeling rocky.
    "I have got saddle galls
    On both of my balls."
But the doctor wrote down: Gonococci.

There was a young girl of Kilkenny
On whose genital parts there were many
    Venereal growths—
    The result of wild oats
Sown there by a fellow named Benny.

There was a young maid of Klepper,
Went out one night with a stepper,
    And now in dismay
    She murmurs each day,
"His pee-pee was made of red-pepper."

The physicians of Countess van Krapp
Found a terrible rash on her map—
    Sores that opened and closed—
    Which they soon diagnosed
As a case of perennial clap.

There was a young lady named Lea
Whose favors were frequent and free,
    And pants-pigeons flew
    Where her gooseberries grew,
And some of them flew onto me.

He'll be there to inspect me,
With a big syringe to inject me—
    Oh, I'll be humpbacked
    Before I get back
To Ten-Ten-Tennessee . . .

There was a young lady of Michigan
Who said, "Damn it! I've got the itch again."
   Said her mother, "That's strange,
   I'm surprised it ain't mange,
If you've slept with that son-of-a-bitch again."

        There was an old man of Molucca
        Who wanted his daughter, to fuck her.
           But she got the best
           Of his little incest,
        And poxed the old man of Molucca.

There was a young lady named Nance
Who had ants in the seat of her pants.
   When they bit her on the bottom
   She yelled, "Jesus God, rot 'em!
I can't do the St. Vitus dance."

There once was a Spanish nobilio
Who lived in a Spanish castilio.
   His cojones grew hot
   Much more often than not
At the thought of a Spanish jazzilio.

The wife of a Viking in Norway
Was caught taking a nap in a doorway.
   "When you make the attack,
   Let it be from the back,
Because lately the front way's the sore way."

Alack, for the doughty O'Connor
Who fucked like a fiend for his honor,
   Till a flapper named Rhea
   Colluded to be a
Mother to Leuco and Gonor.

A charming young lady named Randall
Has a clap that the doctors can't handle.
   So this lovely, lorn floozie,
   With her poor, damaged coosie,
Must take her delight with a candle.

    A rank whore, there ne'er was a ranker,
    Possessed an Hunterian chancre,
      But she made an elision
      By a transverse incision,
    For which all her lovers may thank her.

There was a young lady of Reading
Who got poxed and the virus kept spreading.
   Her nymphae each day
   Kept sloughing away,
Till at last you could shove your whole head in.

A girl to the druggist did say,
"I am bothered with bugs in my hay."
  "I see what you mean,
  You need Paris green
To be rid of the things right away."

The results of this piece of mischance
Were disastrous, you'll see at a glance.
  First died bugs, then went trees,
  Then her pet Pekinese,
And two gentlemen just in from France.

There was a young lady at sea
Who said, "God, how it hurts me to pee."
  "I see," said the mate,
  "That accounts for the state
Of the captain, the purser, and me."

A virile young G. I. named Shorty
Was lively and known to be "sporty."
    But he once made a slip
    And showed up with a "drip,"
And was redlined (35-1440).

      A boy whose skin long I suppose is,
      Was dreadfully ill with phymosis.
        The doctor said, "Why,
        Circumcision we'll try,
      A plan recommended by Moses."

There was an old man of Tantivy
Who followed his son to the privy.
   He lifted the lid
   To see what he did,
And found that it smelt of Capivi.

There was an old man at the Terminus
Whose bush and whose bum were all verminous.
   They said: "You sale Boche!
   You really must wash
Before you start planting your sperm in us."

14
Losses

There was a young lady of Alnwick
Whom a stranger threw into a panic.
    For he frigged her and fucked her,
    And buggered and sucked her,
With a glee hardly short of satanic.

                    There was an old maid from Bermuda
                    Who shot a marauding intruder.
                        It was not her ire
                        At his lack of attire,
                    But he reached for her jewels as he screwed her.

An explorer returned from Australia,
Reported lost paraphernalia:
    A Zeiss microscope
    And his personal hope,
Which had vanished with his genitalia.

There was a young sailor named Bates
Who did the fandango on skates.
   He fell on his cutlass
   Which rendered him nutless
And practically useless on dates.

I lost my arm in the army,
I lost my leg in the navy,
   I lost my balls
   Over Niagara Falls,
And I lost my cock in a lady.

There was a young lady named Perkin
Who swallowed an extra-large gherkin.
   Now she doesn't spend much
   On kotex and such,
On account of her drain isn't workin'.

There was a young man of Porcellian,
A rotter, a shitheel, a hellion.
    But the X-ray revealed
    That his sperm was congealed,
And both of his balls in rebellion.

        A bibulous bishop would preach
        After sunning his balls on the beach.
           But his love life was ended
           By a paunch so distended
        It annulled, ipso facto, his reach.

There was a young fellow named Puttenham
Whose tool caught in doors upon shuttin' 'em.
    He said, "Well, perchance
    It would help to wear pants,
If I just could remember to button 'em."

One evening a workman named Rawls
Fell asleep in his old overalls.
   And when he woke up, he
   Discovered a puppy
Had bitten off both of his balls.

A horny young fellow named Redge
Was jerking off under a hedge.
   The gardener drew near
   With a huge pruning shear,
And trimmed off the edge of his wedge.

There once was a girl at the Ritz
Who liked to have men bite her tits.
   One good Fletcherizer
   Made her sadder but wiser
By chewing them up into bits.

A geologist named Dr. Robb
Was perturbed by his thingamabob,
    So he took up his pick
    And wanged off his wick,
And calmly went on with his job.

There was an old man from Robles
Who went out to dine with some nobles.
    He would risk his life,
    And fucked the host's wife,
And now, so 'tis said, he has no balls.

When the White Man attempted to rule,
The Indians made him a fool.
    They cut off his nuts
    To hang in their huts,
And stuffed up his mouth with his tool.

There was a young fellow named Bill
Who took an atomic pill.
   His navel corroded,
   His asshole exploded,
And they found his nuts in Brazil.

While pissing on deck, an old boatswain
Fell asleep, and his pisser got frozen.
   It snapped at the shank,
   And it fell off and sank
In the sea—'twas his own fault for dozin'.

There was a young fellow named Bob
Who explained to his friends with a sob,
   "The size of my phallus
   Was just right for Alice
Till the night that she bit off the knob."

There was a young fellow from Boston
Who rode around in an Austin.
   There was room for his ass
   And a gallon of gas,
But his balls hung outside, and he lost 'em.

     A miner who bored in Brazil
     Found some very strange rust on his drill.
       He thought it a joke
       Till the bloody thing broke—
     Now his tailings are practically nil.

An eccentric young poet named Brown
Raised up his embroiderèd gown
   To look for his peter
   To beat it to meter,
But fainted when none could be found.

A Bavarian dame named Brunhilde
Went to bed with a jerry-built builder.
    The end of his john
    Was so badly put on
That it snapped in her bladder and killed her.

There was a young man of Calcutta
Who tried to write "cunt" on a shutter.
    He had got to "c-u-"
    When a pious Hindu
Knocked him arse-over-tip in the gutter.

There was a young man of Canute
Who was troubled by warts on his root.
    He put acid on these,
    And now, when he pees,
He can finger his root like a flute.

Another young man, from Beirut,
Played a penis as one might a flute,
    Till he met a sad eunuch
    Who lifted his tunic
And said, "Sir, my instrument's mute."

    There was a young girl in a cast
    Who had an unsavory past,
        For the neighborhood pastor
        Tried fucking through plaster,
    And his very first fuck was his last.

There were two young men of Cawnpore
Who buggered and fucked the same whore.
    But the partition split,
    And the gism and shit
Rolled out in great lumps on the floor.

The wife of a red-headed Celt
Lost the key to her chastity belt.
  She tried picking the lock
  With an Ulsterman's cock,
And the next thing he knew, he was gelt.

There was an old lady of Cheadle
Who sat down in church on a needle.
  The needle, though blunt,
  Penetrated her cunt,
But was promptly removed by the beadle.

The wife of an athlete named Chuck
Found her married life shit-out-of-luck.
  Her husband played hockey
  Without wearing a jockey—
Now he hasn't got what it takes for a fuck.

There was a young lady of Clewer
Who was riding a bike, and it threw her.
  A man saw her there
  With her legs in the air,
And seized the occasion to screw her.

There was a young man of Coblenz
The size of whose balls was immense.
   One day, playing soccer,
   He sprung his left knocker,
And kicked it right over the fence.

An unfortunate bugger named Cowl
Took a shit while as drunk as an owl.
   He stumbled, alack!
   And fell flat on his back,
And his ballocks slipped into his bowel.

There was a young girl from the Creek
Who had her period twice every week.
   "How very provoking,"
   Said the Vicar from Woking,
"There's no time for poking, so to speak."

The wife of a chronic crusader
Took on every man who waylaid her,
   Till the amorous itch
   Of this popular bitch
So annoyed the crusader he spayed her.

There was a young lady of Dee
Who went down to the river to swim.
   A man in a punt
   Stuck an oar in her eye,
And now she wears glasses, you see.

There was a young fellow named Dick
Who was cursed with a spiralling prick,
   So he set out to hunt
   For a screw-twisted cunt
That would match with his corkscrewy dick.

There was a young singer named Springer,
Got his testicles caught in the wringer.
   He hollered with pain,
   As they rolled down the drain,
(Falsetto): "There goes my career as a singer!"

There was a young girl named Dinwiddie
With a brace of voluptuous titty.
    But the boys squeezed them so
    That they hung down below,
And one drooped behind and got shitty.

        There was a young lady named Dowd
        Whom a young fellow groped in the crowd.
            But the thing that most vexed her
            Was that when he stood next her
        He said, "How's your cunt?" right out loud.

There was a young lady named Duff
With a lovely, luxuriant muff.
    In his haste to get in her,
    One eager beginner
Lost both of his balls in the rough.

There was a young lady named Eva
Who went to a ball as Godiva,
   But a change in the lights
   Showed a tear in her tights,
And a low fellow present yelled, "Beaver!"

There was an old fellow of Ewing
Who said: "It's computing I'm doing.
   By leaving my drawers on
   While clambering whores, on
The whole I've lost ten miles of screwing."

There was a man from Far Rockaway
Who could skizzle a broad from a block away.
   Once while taking a fuck,
   Along came a truck
And knocked both his balls and his cock away.

And then there's a story that's fraught
With disaster—of balls that got caught
  When a chap took a crap
  In the woods, and a trap
Underneath . . . Oh, I can't bear the thought!

A careless old hooker in Frisco
Got turpentine mixed in her pisco
  And scalded with steam
  A muff-diver's dream
Because he refused to let puss go.

There was a young man from Glenchasm
Who had a tremendous orgasm.
  In the midst of his thralls
  He burst both his balls
And covered an acre with plasm.

There was an old person of Gosham
Who took out his ballocks to wash 'em.
   His wife said, "Now, Jack,
    If you don't put them back,
I'll step on your scrotum and squash 'em."

A gallant young Frenchman named Grandhomme
Was attempting a girl on a tandem.
   At the height of the make
   She slammed on the brake,
And scattered his semen at random.

There was a young lady named Hall,
Wore a newspaper dress to a ball.
   The dress caught on fire
   And burned her entire
Front page, sporting section, and all.

There was an old sheik named Al Hassid
Whose tool had become very placid.
   Before each injection,
   To get an erection
He had to immerse it in acid.

      There was a young man in Havana,
      Fucked a girl on a player piano.
         At the height of their fever
           Her ass hit the lever—
      Yes! He has no banana!

I'm only a sterilized heiress,
A butt for the laughter of rubes.
   I'm comely and rich,
   But a venomous bitch—
My mother—ran off with my tubes.

There was a young man with a hernia
Who said to his surgeon, "Gol-dernya,
  When carving my middle,
  Be sure you don't fiddle
With matters that do not concern ya."

A marine being sent to Hong Kong
Got his doctor to alter his dong.
  He sailed off with a tool
  Flat and thin as a rule—
When he got there he found he was wrong.

There was a young fellow named Hyde
Who took a girl out for a ride.
  He mucked up her fuckhole
  And fucked up her muckhole,
And charged her two dollars beside.

Consider the case of Charles the Insane
Who had a large cock and a very small brain.
　　While fucking his sister
　　He raised a large blister
On the tip of his whip and her pubic terrain.

　　　　　There was a young Scotchman named Jock
　　　　　Who had the most horrible shock:
　　　　　　　He once took a shit
　　　　　　　In a leaf-covered pit,
　　　　　And the crap sprung a trap on his cock.

The conquering Lion of Judah
Made a prayer to the statue of Buddha.
　　"Oh, Idol," he prayed,
　　"May Il Duce be spayed,
And all his descendants be neuter!"

There was a young couple named Kelly
Who had to live belly to belly,
   Because once, in their haste,
   They used library paste
Instead of petroleum jelly.

There was a young man of Khartoum
Who lured a poor girl to her doom.
   He not only fucked her,
   But buggered and sucked her—
And left her to pay for the room.

Said old Mr. Wellington Koo:
"Now what in the Hell shall I do?
   My wife is too hot,
   I can't fill up her slot."
So he screwed her to bits trying to.

A crooner who lived in Lahore
Got his balls caught in a door.
   Now his mezzo soprano
   Is rather piano,
Though he was a loud basso before.

        There was a young Marquis of Landsdowne
        Who tried hard to keep his great stands down.
           Said he, "But that I thought
           I should break it off short,
        My penis I'd hold with both hands down."

Did you hear about young Henry Lockett?
He was blown down the street by a rocket.
   The force of the blast
   Blew his balls up his ass,
And his pecker was found in his pocket.

There was a young girl named Louise
With a marvelous vaginal squeeze.
    She inspired such pleasure
    In her lover's yard measure
That she caused his untimely decease.

There was a young man of Madras
Who was fucking a girl in the grass,
    But the tropical sun
    Spoiled half of his fun
By singeing the hair off his ass.

There was a young man of Malacca
Who always slept on his left knacker.
    One Saturday night
    He slept on his right,
And his knacker went off like a cracker.

Growing tired of her husband's great mass,
A young bride inserted some glass.
    The prick of her hubby
    Is now short and stubby,
While the wife can now piss through her ass.

    A girl of as graceful a mien
    As ever in London was seen
        Stepped into a pub,
        Hit her man with a club,
    And razored to shreds his machine.

There was a young man of Missouri
Who fucked with a terrible fury,
    Till hauled into court
    For his bestial sport,
And condemned by a poorly hung jury.

All winter the eunuch from Munich
Went walking in naught but a tunic.
   Folks said, "You've a cough;
   You'll freeze your balls off!"
Said he, "That's why I'm a eunuch."

There was a young lady named Nance
Whose lover had St. Vitus dance.
   When she dove for his prick,
   He wriggled so quick,
She bit a piece out of his pants.

There was a young lady in Natchez
Who fell in some nettle-wood patches.
   She sits in her room
   With her bare little moon,
And scratches, and scratches, and scratches.

There was an old man from New York
Whose tool was as dry as a cork.
    While attempting to screw,
    He split it in two,
And now his tool is a fork.

A bridegroom at Niagara Falls,
His fate was sad, and it appalls—
    His bride refused to fuck him,
    Or bugger, frig, or suck him—
So he went nuts—cut off his putz
And then bit off his balls.

When Abelard near Notre Dame
Had taught his fair pupil the game,
    Her uncle—the wag—
    Cut off Peter's bag,
And his lectures were never the same.

A young man of Novorossisk
Had a mating procedure so brisk,
   With such superspeed action
   The Lorentz contraction
Foreshortened his prick to a disk.

There once was a Frenchman from Pau
Who went for a slide on the snow.
   He traveled so fast
   That he skinned off his ass,
And the cuticle now has to grow.

A nudist by name Roger Peet
Loved to dance in the snow and the sleet,
   But one chilly December
   He froze every member,
And retired to a monkish retreat.

15

Sex Substitutes

A man in the battle of Aix
Had one nut and his cock shot away,
    But found out in this pickle
    His nose could still tickle,
Though he might get the snuffles some day.

        Nymphomaniacal Alice
        Used a dynamite stick for a phallus.
           They found her vagina
           In North Carolina,
        And her asshole in Buckingham Palace.

A lesbian lassie named Anny
Desired to appear much more manny,
    So she whittled a pud
    Of mahogany wood,
And let it protrude from her cranny.

There once was a young Aztec
Who was fond of reading Steinbeck.
When asked where she read,
She said, "Always in bed,
Especially when wearing Kotex."

There was a young man of Bagdad
Who was dreaming that he was a shad.
He dreamt he was spawning,
And then, the next morning,
He found that, by Jesus! he had.

There was a young man of Balbriggan
Who was fearfully given to frigging,
Till these nocturnal frolics
Played hell with his bollocks,
And killed the young man of Balbriggan.

An eunuch frequenting Bangkok
Used to borrow the deified jock
From a local rain god
When he went for a prod—
You could hear the girl yell for a block.

When a girl, young Elizabeth Barrett,
Was found by her ma in a garret,
    She had shoved up a diamond
    As far as her hymen,
And was ramming it home with a carrot.

There was a young girl of Batonger,
Used to diddle herself with a conger.
    When asked how it feels
    To be pleasured by eels,
She said, "Just like a man, only longer."

A nudist resort at Benares
Took a midget in all unawares.
    But he made members weep
    For he just couldn't keep
His nose out of private affairs.

There was a young man from Bengal
Who got in a hole in the wall.
    "Oh," he sad, "It's a pity
    This hole is so glitty,
But it's better than nothing at all."

There was an asexual bigot
Whose cock only served as a spigot,
  Till a jolly young whore
  Taught him tricks by the score;
Now his greatest delight is to frig it.

There once was a horny old bitch
With a motorized self-fucker which
  She would use with delight
  All day long and all night—
Twenty bucks: Abercrombie & Fitch.

There was a young man of Bombay
Who fashioned a cunt out of clay,
  But the heat of his prick
  Turned it into a brick,
And chafed all his foreskin away.

A squeamish young fellow named Brand
Thought caressing his penis was grand,
    But he viewed with distaste
    The gelatinous paste
That it left in the palm of his hand.

        There was a young fellow named Bream
        Who never had dreamt a wet dream,
           For when lacking a whore
           He'd just bore out the core
        Of an apple and fuck it through cream.

There was a young man from the Bronx
Who when offered a piece said, "No thonx."
    He said, "I declare,
    I prefer solitaire,
And all that I do is just yonx."

There was a young naval cadet
Whose dreams were unusually wet.
    When he dreamt of his wedding,
    He soaked up the bedding,
And the wedding ain't taken place yet.

There was a young man of Calcutta
Who jerked himself off in the gutter,
    But the tropical sun
    Played hell with his gun
And turned all his cream into butter.

A young jacker-off of Cawnpore
Never felt a desire for more.
    In bold self-reliance
    He cried out his defiance
Of the joys of the fairy and whore.

There was a young fellow named Chisholm
Afflicted with skin erotism.
   In bathing, he'd rub
   His prick in the tub
Till the water was soapy with jism.

        There was a young girl of Cohoes
        Who jerked herself off with her nose.
           She said, "Yes, I done it,
           But just for the fun it
        Afforded the folk of Cohoes."

There once was a fabulous Creole
Whose prick had a wide-open peehole.
   This carrot so orange
   Got caught in the door hinge
When he tried to bugger the keyhole.

There was a young woman of Croft
Who played with herself in a loft,
   Having reasoned that candles
    Could never cause scandals,
Besides which they did not go soft.

Said another young woman of Croft,
Amusing herself in the loft,
   "A salami or wurst
   Is what I would choose first—
With bologna you know you've been boffed."

There was a young lady of Dallas,
Invented a singular phallus.
   It came and it went,
   And when it was spent,
It proceeded to fill up the chalice.

There was a young fellow from Dallas
Who enjoyed doing things with his phallus.
   So many tricks did he try
   It became, by and by,
Little more than a leather-tough callus.

        There was a young man from Darjeeling
        Whose dong reached up to the ceiling.
           In the electric light socket
           He'd put it and rock it—
        Oh God! What a wonderful feeling!

A geneticist living in Delft
Scientifically played with himself,
   And when he was done
   He labeled it: Son,
And filed him away on the shelf.

A certain young fellow named Dick
Liked to feel a girl's hand on his prick.
   He taught them to fool
   With his rigid old tool
Till the cream shot out, white and thick.

An agreeable girl named Miss Doves
Likes to jack off the young men she loves.
   She will use her bare fist
   If the fellows insist,
But she really prefers to wear gloves.

A lecherous Northumbrian druid,
Whose mind was filthy and lewd,
   Awoke from a trance
   With his hand in his pants
On a lump of pre-seminal fluid.

There was an old Chinaman drunk
Who went for a sail in his junk.
   He was dreaming of Venus
   And tickling his penis,
Till he floated away in the spunk.

There was a young man from Oswego
Who fell in love with a Dago.
    He dreamt that his Venus
    Was jerking his penis,
And woke up all covered with sago.

There was a gay Countess of Dufferin.
One night while her husband was covering,
    Just to chaff him a bit
    She said, "You old shit,
I can buy a dildo for a sovereign."

    The modern cinematic emporium
    Is by no means the merest sexorium
        But a highly effectual
        Heterosexual
    Mutual masturbatorium.

As Apollo was chasing the fair
Daphne she vanished in air.
    He could find but a shrub
    With thick bark on the hub
And not even a knothole to spare.

There were three young ladies of Fetters,
Annoyed all their elders and betters
   By stuffing their cock holders
   With proxies for stockholders,
Old bills, and anonymous letters.

There was a young parson of Goring
Who made a small hole in the flooring.
   He lined it all round,
   Then laid on the ground
And declared it was cheaper than whoring.

A fair-haired young damsel named Grace
Thought it very, very foolish to place
   Her hand on your cock
   When it turned hard as rock,
For fear it would explode in her face.

There was a young lady of Harrow
Who complained that her cunt was too narrow,
    For times without number
    She would use a cucumber,
But could not accomplish a marrow.

        There was a young parson of Harwich,
        Tried to grind his betrothed in a carriage.
            She said, "No, you young goose,
            Just try self-abuse,
        And the other we'll try after marriage."

There was a young lady named Hatch
Who doted on music by Bach.
    She played with her pussy
    To "The Faun" by Debussy,
But to ragtime she just scratched her snatch.

There was a young man from Havana
Who continually played the "piana."
   'Til one day his finger slipped,
   And his fly it ripped,
And out slipped a hairy banana.

A water pipe suited Miss Hunt,
Who used it for many a bunt,
   But the unlucky wench
   Got it caught in her trench—
It took twenty-two men and a big Stillson wrench
To get the thing out of her cunt.

At Vassar sex isn't injurious,
Though of love we are never penurious.
   Thanks to vulcanized aids,
   Though we may die old maids,
At least we shall never die curious.

The swaggering hips of a jade
Raised the cock of a clerical blade.
   Hell-bent for his fun,
   He went home on the run,
And diddled his grandmother's maid.

        A neurotic young man of Kildare
        Drilled a hole in the seat of a chair.
           He fucked it all night,
           Then died of the fright
        That maybe he wasn't "all there."

There was a young lady from Kincaid
Who covered it up with a Band-Aid.
   The boyfriend said, "Shit,
   I can't find the slit!"
And helped himself out with a hand-aid.

An amorous Jew, on Yom Kippur,
Saw a shiksel—decided to clip her.
  "I'll grip her, and strip her,
   And lip her, and whip her—"
Then his dingus shot off in his zipper!

There was a young fellow named Klotz
Who went looking for tail in New Lots.
  Of tail he found nary
  A piece, but a fairy
Suggested he try some ersatz.

There was a young man of Kutki
Who could blink himself off with one eye.
  For a while though, he pined
  When his organ declined
To function, because of a stye.

Since the girl found no joys in her lap,
Pete chopped off her big brother's tap.
   At his death she did not repent
   But fixed it with cement
And wore it in place with a strap.

     An innocent boy in Lapland
     Was told that frigging was grand.
        But at his first trial
        He said with a smile,
     "I've had the same feeling by hand."

She made a thing of soft leather
And topped off the end with a feather.
   When she poked it inside her,
   She took off like a glider
And gave up her lover forever.

There is a young fellow from Leeds
Whose skin is so thin his cocks bleeds
   Whenever erect.
   This dermal defect
Often scares him from sowing his seeds.

There was a young fellow from Lees
Who handled his tool with great ease.
   This continual friction
   Made his sex a mere fiction,
But the callus hangs down to his knees.

There was a young man from Liberia
Who was groping a wench from Nigeria.
   He said, "Say, my pet,
   Your panties are wet."
"Sorry, sir, that's my interior."

There was a pianist named Liszt
Who played with one hand while he pissed,
    But as he grew older
    His technique grew bolder,
And in concert jacked off with his fist.

There was an old parson of Lundy,
Fell asleep in his vestry on Sunday.
    He awoke with a scream:
    "What, another wet dream!
This comes of not frigging since Monday."

A soldier named Dougall McDougall
Was caught jacking off in his bugle.
    Said they of the army,
    "We think that you're barmy,"
Said he, "It's the new way to frugle."

A thrifty old man named McEwen
Inquired: "Why be bothered with screwing?
   It's safer and cleaner
   To finger your wiener,
And besides you can see what you're doing."

There was a young man from McGill
Who was always seen walking uphill.
   When someone inquired,
   "My man, aren't you tired?"
He said, "No, it makes my balls thrill."

There was a young man named McGurk
Who dozed off one night after work.
   He had a wet dream
   But awoke with a scream
Just in time to give it a jerk.

Have you heard of Professor MacKay
Who lays all the girls in the hay?
   Though he thinks it's romantic
   He drives them all frantic
By talking a wonderful lay.

      A horny young girl of Madras
      Reclined with a monk in the grass.
         She tickled his cock
         With the end of a rock
      Till it foamed like a bottle of Bass.

Another young lady named Hicks
Spent all her time thinking of pricks,
   And it was her odd whim
   To tickle her quim
Till it foamed like a bottle of Dick's.

A lusty young woodsman of Maine
For years with no woman had lain,
    But he found sublimation
    At a high elevation
In the crotch of a pine—God, the pain!

There was a young lady named Mandel
Who caused quite a neighborhood scandal
    By coming out bare
    On the main village square
And frigging herself with a candle.

There was a young girl named Maxine
Whose vagina was wondrously clean:
    With her uterus packed,
    She kept safe from attack
With a dill pickle, papulose, green.

There was a young lady named May
Who frigged herself in the hay.
　　She bought a pickle—
　　One for a nickel—
And wore all the warts away!

　　　　In all of the Grecian metropolis
　　　　There was only one virgin—Papapoulos;
　　　　　　But her cunt was all callous
　　　　　　From fucking the phallus
　　　　Of a god that adorned the Acropolis.

There were two Greek girls of Miletus
Who said, "We wear gadgets that treat us,
　　When strapped on the thigh
　　Up cozy and high,
To constant, convenient coitus."

There was an aesthetic young Miss
Who thought it the apex of bliss
　　To jazz herself silly
　　With the bud of a lily,
Then go to the garden and piss.

There was a young girl of Mobile
Whose hymen was made of chilled steel,
　　To give her a thrill
　　Took a rotary drill
Or a number nine emery wheel.

There was a young man from Montrose
Who could diddle himself with his toes.
　　He did it so neat
　　He fell in love with his feet,
And christened them Myrtle and Rose.

Oh, that supple young man of Montrose
Who tickled his tail with his toes!
    His landlady said,
    As she made up his bed,
"My God! How that man blows his nose!"

There was a young lady from Munich
Who was had in a park by a eunuch.
    In a moment of passion
    He shot her a ration
From a squirt gun concealed 'neath his tunic.

There was a young girl from New York
Who diddled herself with a cork.
    It stuck in her vagina—
    Can you imagina
Prying it out with a fork!

16

Eccentricities

There was a young lady of Asia
Who had an odd kind of aphasia.
   She'd forget that her cunt
   Was located in front,
Which deprived her of most of the pleasure.

     There was a young queen of Baroda
     Who built a new kind of pagoda.
        The walls of its halls
        Were festooned with the balls
     And the tools of the fools that bestrode her.

There was a young man of Australia
Who painted his ass like a dahlia.
   The drawing was fine,
   The color divine,
The scent—ah, that was a failure.

A lecherous fellow named Babbitt
Asked a girl if she'd fuck or would nab it.
   Said she, "From long habit
   I fuck like a rabbit,
So I'd rather cohabit than grab it."

A reformer who went out to Bali
To change the sartorial folly
   Of the girls now admits,
   "A pair of good tits
In season can seem rather jolly."

There was a young girl of Asturias
With a penchant for practices curious.
    She loved to bat rocks
    With her gentlemen's cocks—
A practice both rude and injurious.

There was a young fellow of Barrow
Whose whang bone was lacking in marrow.
    To accomplish a rape,
    He wound it in tape
And feathered the shaft like an arrow.

The Reverend Henry Ward Beecher
Called a girl a most elegant creature.
    So she laid on her back
    And, exposing her crack,
Said, "Fuck that, you old Sunday school teacher!"

There was a young man of Belgravia
Who cared neither for God nor his Savior.
    He walked down the Strand
    With his prick in his hand
And was jailed for indecent behavior.

      A vigorous fellow named Bert
      Was attracted by every new skirt.
         Oh, it wasn't their minds
         But their rounded behinds
      That excited this lovable flirt.

A lazy, fat fellow named Betts
Upon his fat ass mostly sets.
    Along comes a gal
    And says, "I'll fuck you, pal."
Says he, "If you'll do the work, let's."

There was a young fellow named Bliss
Whose sex life was strangely amiss,
    For even with Venus
    His recalcitrant penis
Would never do better than this.

There once was an actress of Bonely,
And the men never let her be lonely.
    So she hung out in front
    Of her popular cunt
A sign reading, "Standing Room Only."

There was a gay Countess of Bray,
And you may think it odd when I say,
    That in spite of high station,
    Rank, and education,
She always spelt "cunt" with a "k."

There was a young lady in Brent,
When her old man's pecker, it bent,
  She said with a sigh,
  "Oh, why must it die?
Let's fill it with Portland cement."

There was a young lady named Bruce
Who captured her man by a ruse;
  She filled up her fuselage
  With a good grade of mucilage,
And he never could pry himself loose.

There was an old man from Bubungi
Whose balls were all covered with fungi.
  With his friends, out at lunch,
  He tore off a bunch
And said, "Now divide this among ye."

On a bridge sat the Bishop of Buckingham
Thinking of twats and of sucking 'em,
   And watching the stunts
   Of the cunts in the punts,
And the tricks of the pricks that were fucking 'em.

There was a young maid of Cardiff,
Whose father one day asked if
   To church she would walk
   To hear some good talk,
When the young maid replied, "Ax my spiff."

On guard by the bridge of Carquinez
With his eyes on the evening star, Venus,
   With the sky full of blimps,
   And the town full of pimps,
And an incredible length in his penis.

There was a young fellow named Chick
Who fancied himself rather slick.
   He went to a ball
   Dressed in nothing at all
But a big velvet bow round his prick.

There was a young lady from China
Who mistook for her mouth her vagina.
   Her clitoris huge
   She covered with rouge
And lipsticked her labia minor.

The ancient orthographer Chisholm
Caused a lexicographical schism
   When he asked to know whether
   'Twere known which was better
To use—"g" or "j"—to spell "jism."

There was a young man from the Coast
Who received a parcel by post.
   It contained, so I heard,
   A triangular turd
And the balls of his grandfather's ghost.

There was a young girl of Connecticut
Who didn't care much about etiquette.
   Whenever she was able
   She'd piss on the table,
And mop off her cunt with her petticoat.

An ignorant maiden named Crewe-Pitt
Did something amazingly stupid:
   When her lover had spent
   She douched with cement,
And gave birth to a statue of Cupid.

The Duchess of Drood's lewd and crude,
And the men think her terribly rude.
    When they swim by the docks,
    She tickles their cocks
And laughs when the red tips protrude.

    A certain young lady named Daisy
    Who is really infernally lazy
        Said, "I haven't the time
        To wipe my behine,
    But the way I can hump drives 'em crazy."

There was a shy boy named Dan
Who tickled his girl with a fan.
    She started to flirt,
    So he lifted her skirt
And gave her a fuck like a man.

There was a young man of Datchet
Who cut off his prick with a hatchet,
    Then very politely
    He sent it to Whitely,
And ordered a cunt that would match it.

Meat rationing did not terrify Miss Davey.
She got married to a sailor in the Navy,
    For she knew between his legs
    He had ham and he had eggs,
A big wienie, and oodles of white gravy.

There was a young priest named Delaney
Who said to the girls, "Nota bene,
    I've seen how you swish up
    Your skirts at the bishop
Whenever the weather is rainy."

A surly and pessimist druid,
A defeatist, if only he knew it,
　　Said, "The world's on the skids,
　　And I think having kids
Is a waste of good seminal fluid."

　　　　The grand-niece of Madame DuBarry
　　　　Suspected her son was a toy.
　　　　　"It's peculiar," said she,
　　　　　"But he sits down to pee,
　　　　And stands when I bathe the canary."

In his garden remarked Lord Dunedin:
"A fig for your diggin' and weedin'.
　　I like watching birds
　　While they're dropping their turds,
And spyin' on guinea pigs breedin'."

I dined with the Duchess of Dyches,
Who said, "God! how my bottom hole itches!"
　　So she passed around switches
　　And took down her britches,
And soon her dinner guests had her in stitches.

There was a young girl of East Anglia
Whose loins were a tangle of ganglia.
　Her mind was a webbing
　Of Freud and Krafft-Ebing
And all sorts of other newfanglia.

Said Einstein, "I have an equation
Which science might call Rabelaisian.
　　Let "P" be virginity
　　Approaching infinity,
And "U" be a constant, persuasion.

A pretty young girl Eskimo
Thought it very patriotic to sew
    Ballock-warmers for those
    Who were fighting the foes,
And on whom the North wind would blow.

    There was a young man from Eurasia
    Who toasted his balls in a brazier
        Till they grew quite as hot
        As the glamorous twat
    Of Miss Brenda Diana Duff Frazier.

A psychoneurotic fanatic
Said: "I take little girls to the attic,
    Then whistle a tune
    'Bout the cow and the moon—
When the cow jumps, I come. It's dramatic."

There was an old fellow named Fletcher,
A lewd and perverted old lecher.
 In a spirit of meanness
 He cut off his penis,
And now he regrets it, I betcha.

A mystical painter named Foxx
Once picked up a girl on the docks.
 He made an elliptic
 Mysterious triptych,
And painted it right on her box.

There was a young cowboy named Gary
Who was morbidly anxious to marry,
 But he found the defection
 Of any erection
A difficult factor to parry.

A proper young person named Gissing
Announced he had given up kissing.
   "I strike out at once
   For something that counts,
And besides, my girl's front teeth are missing."

      A young baseball fan named Miss Glend
      Was the home-team's best rooter and friend,
         But for her the big league
         Never held the intrigue
      Of a bat with two balls at the end.

I love her in her evening gown,
I love her in her nightie,
   But when moonlight flits
   Between her tits,
Jesus Christ, almighty!

The favorite pastime of grandfather
Was tickling his balls with a feather.
   But the thing he liked best
   Of all the rest
Was knocking them gently together.

A company of Grenadier Guards,
While traversing the park, formed in squads,
   Saw two naked statues
   At three-quarter pratt views,
Which perceptibly stiffened their rods.

There was a young athlete named Grimmon
Who developed a new way of swimmin':
   By a marvellous trick
   He would scull with his prick,
Which attracted loud cheers from the women.

An old Jap samurai named Haki
Once pickled his penis in saki.
When the thing was quite dead,
He cried with bowed head:
"Banzai! Requiescat in pace."

A Biblical party called Ham
Cried: "Cuss it, I don't give a damn!
My father's yard measure
I view with great pleasure,
Such a bloody great battering ram!"

There once was a lady handletterer
Who thought of a program to better her.
She handlettered each
Of the parts she could reach—
The bosoms, the navel, et cetera.

There was a young girlie named Hannah
Who loved madly her lover's banana.
    She loved pubic hair
    And balls that were bare,
And she jacked him off in her bandana.

A sensitive fellow named Harry
Thought sex too revolting to marry.
    So he went out in curls
    And frowned on the girls,
And he got to be known as a fairy.

A fine Southern lady named Hentz
Preferred colored boys when she'd yentz.
    She explained, "When they're black,
    They've a spring in their back,
And their tools are most always immense."

An ingenious young fellow named Herman
Tied a bow on the end of his worm, and
   His wife said, "How festive!"
   But he said, "Don't be restive—
You'll wriggle it off with your squirmin'."

        There was an announcer named Herschel
        Whose habits became controversial,
           Because when out wooing
           Whatever he was doing,
        At ten he'd insert his commercial.

There was a young lady named Hicks
Who delighted to play with men's pricks,
   Which she would embellish
   With evident relish,
And make them stand up and do tricks.

There was a young girl from Hong Kong
Whose cervical cap was a gong.
   She said with a yell
   As a shot rang the bell,
"I'll give you a ding for a dong."

There was a young man in Hong Kong
Who grew seven fathoms of prong.
   It looked, when erect,
   About as you'd expect—
When coiled, it did not seem so long.

There was a young man named Ignatius
Who lived in a garret quite spacious.
   When he went to his auntie's
   He always wore panties,
But alone in his garret—good gracious!

There was a sad prude out in Iowa
Who would say: "Please say it my way:
   Do not say fuck,
   It don't rime with duck.
Say untcay and itshay and uckfay."

A sweet young strip dancer named Jane
Wore five inches of thin cellophane.
   When asked why she wore it,
   She said, "I abhor it,
But my cunt juice would spatter like rain."

17
Women

There was a young woman from Aenos
Who came to our party as Venus.
  We told her how rude
  'Twas to come there quite nude,
And we brought her a leaf from the green-h'us.

There was an old man of Boolong
Who frightened the birds with his song.
  It wasn't the words
  That frightened the birds
But the horrible dooble ong-tong.

A lady athletic and handsome
Got wedged in her sleeping room transom.
   When she offered much gold
   For release, she was told
That the view was worth more than the ransom.

A fanatic gun-lover named Crust
Was perverse to the point of disgust.
   His idea of a peach
   Had a sixteen-inch breech,
And a pearl-handled 44 bust.

A daring young maid from Dubuque
Risked a rather decided rebuke
   By receiving a prude
   In the absolute nude,
But he gasped, "If you only could cook!"

A wonderful fish is the flea,
He bores and he bites on me.
   I would love, indeed,
   To watch him feed,
But he bites me where I cannot see.

A girl attending Bryn Mawr
Committed a dreadful faux pas.
   She loosened a stay
   In her décolleté,
Exposing her je-ne-sais-quoi.

      There was a young lady of Joppa
      Who came a society cropper.
         She went to Ostend
         With a gentleman friend—
      The rest of the story's improper.

There was a young girl of Oak Knoll
Who thought it exceedingly droll
   At a masquerade ball
   Dressed in nothing at all
To back in as a Parker House roll.

      The cross-eyed old painter McNeff
      Was color-blind, palsied, and deaf.
         When he asked to be touted,
         The critics all shouted,
      "This is art, with a capital F!"

There was a young maid from Madras
Who had a magnificent ass;
   Not rounded and pink,
   As you probably think—
It was grey, had long ears, and ate grass.

      In La France once a clevair young man
      Met a girl on the beach down at Cannes.
        Said the mademoiselle,
        "Eh, m'sieu, vot ze 'ell?
      Stay away where eet ees not son-tan!"

There was a young maid of Boston, Mass.,
Who stood in the water up to her knees.
   (If it doesn't rhyme now,
It will when the tide comes in.)

      There was an old sculptor named Phidias
      Whose knowledge of art was invidious.
        He carved Aphrodite
        Without any nightie—
      Which startled the purely fastidious.

There's a man in the Bible portrayed
As one deeply engrossed in his trade.
   He became quite elated
   Over things he created,
Especially the women he made.

      A king sadly said to his queen,
      "In parts you have grown far from lean."
         "I don't give a damn,
          You've always liked ham,"
      She replied, and he gasped, "How obscene!"

A bather, whose clothing was strewed
By winds that left her quite nude,
   Saw a man come along,
   And unless we are wrong,
You expected this line to be lewd.

      I sat next to the Duchess at tea.
      It was just as I feared it would be:
         Her rumblings abdominal
         Were simply phenomenal,
      And everyone thought it was me!

There's a sensitive man in Tom's River
Whom Minsky's causes to quiver.
   The aesthetic vibration
   Brings soulful elation,
And also is good for the liver.

       There was a young person of Tottenham
       Whose manners, Good Lord! she'd forgotten 'em.
          When she went to the vicar's,
          She took off her knickers,
       Because she said she was hot in 'em.

There was a young lady of Trent
Who said that she knew what it meant
   When he asked her to dine—
   Private room, lots of wine,
She knew, oh she knew!—but she went!

There once was a fellow named Trete
Who from birth was inclined to be neat.
   He became extra fussy
   When he thought his pants mussy,
And would throw them away in the street.

A handsome young widow named Vi
Seduced all the wardens nearby.
   When the siren said, "Woo!"
   What else could they do
To extinguish the gleam in her eye?

There was a young lady from Waste
Who fled from a man in some haste.
   She tripped as she ran,
   And fell flat on her pan—
She sometimes still dreams that she's chaste.

18

Horrors

A young man from famed Chittagong
Worked hard at the stool and worked long.
   He felt a hard mass
   Obstructing his ass,
Then shit and cried, "I shit a gong!"

       There once was a gangster named Brown,
       The wiliest bastard in town.
          He was caught by the G-men
          Shooting his semen
       Where the cops would all slip and fall down.

There was a cute quirp from Calcutta
Who was fond of churning love butta.
   One night she was heard to mutta
   That her quim was a-flutta
For the thing she called "Utterly-Utta!"

An unfortunate fellow named Chase
Had an ass that was not quite in place,
   And he showed indignation
   When an investigation
Showed that some people shit through their face.

A plump English prof, from Atlanta
Was bloated with bawdy, bold banter.
   He'd sit on his ass
   And let fly his gas
Whenever he sniffed a decanter.

There was a stout lady of Cuttack,
Posteriorly pecked by a wild duck,
 Who pursued her for miles
 And continued his wiles
Till he completely demolished her buttock.

It was on the 7th of December
That Franklin D. took out his member.
 He said, like the bard:
 "It will be long and very hard.
Pearl Harbor has given me something to
remember."

There was a young fellow from Eno
Who said to his girl, "Now, old Beano,
 Lift your skirt up in front,
 And enlarge your old cunt,
For the size of this organ is keen-o."

A maiden who dwells in Galena
Has bubbies of graceful demeanor,
    And whenever she preens
    These astounding poitrines,
She insists upon Simoniz Kleener.

    It's a helluva fix that we're in
    When the geographical spread of the urge to sin
        Causes juvenile delinquency
        With increasing frequency
    By the Army, the Navy, and Errol Flynn.

To Italy went Sinclair Lewis,
Documenting the life led by loose
    American drunks,
    But he unpacked his trunks
'Cause Florence slipped him a goose.

    There was a young fellow named Louvies
    Who tickled his girl in the boovies,
        And as she contorted,
        He looked down and snorted,
    "My prick wants to get in your movies!"

A person of most any nation,
If afflicted with bad constipation,
   Can shove a cuirass
   Up the crack of his ass,
But it isn't a pleasing sensation.

I got this from the fellow what own it;
He declared that he boasted one mo' nut
   Than most people sport,
   But was terribly short
In the part you might stick through a doughnut.

Said my wife as she stood on a rostrum,
"I don't mind if I don't have colostrum,
   But I'll take an option
   If your child's for adoption—
Though I cannot bear kids, I can foster 'em."

There was a young man in Schenectady,
And he found it quite hard to erect, said he,
   Till he took an injection
   For deficient erection,
Which in just the desired way affected he!

There was a young student of Skat, ah me!
Who said, "What have these wenches got o' me?
 I have lost father's knees,
 Likewise my pancreas,
And I fear I shall die of phlebotomy."

An untutored Southwestern solon
Couldn't tell his behind from a hole in
 That good Texas ground
 Till the day that he found
That oil wouldn't come out of his colon.

A hopeful young lady of Sukker Barrage
Possessed a big swelling she hoped would assuage.
 On her way to the train,
 She was caught in the rain—
Oh, what a sad tale of hopeless Miss Carriage!

A horrid old lady of Summit,
Every time she got laid had to vomit,
    And although she would groan
    When her man got a bone,
"Give it here," she would say, "and I'll gum it."

There was a young girl from Vistula
To whom a friend said, "Jeff has kissed you, la!"
    Said she, "Yes, by God!
    But my arse he can't sod,
Because I am troubled with fistula."

There was a young man from Wanamee
Well schooled in the technique of sodomy.
    He buggered with glee
    An old man in a tree,
And remarked with a shrug, "Won't you pardon me?"

Said a platinum blonde from Warsaw,
As she looked at herself in the raw,
   "'Neath my umbilicus
   (And as like Mike as Ike is)
There's a picture of George Bernard Shaw."

        A bishop there was of Pyongyang
        Who offered an actress his dong.
           She cried, "'Pon my Seoul,
           I have a huge hole,
        But your thing's just comme-ci Kumsong."

There was a young man from Saskatchewan
Whose pecker was truly gargantuan.
   It was good for large whores
   And small dinosaurs,
And sufficiently rough to scratch a match upon.